Help
in the
Classroom

Margaret H. Balshaw

David Fulton Publishers

London

David Fulton Publishers Ltd
2 Barbon Close, London WC1N 3JX

First published in Great Britain by
David Fulton Publishers 1991

Note: The right of Margaret H. Balshaw to be identified as the author of this work has been
asserted by her in accordance with the Copyright, Designs and Patents Act 1988.

Copyright © Margaret H. Balshaw

British Library Cataloguing in Publication Data
Balshaw, M. H.
  Help in the classroom.
  I. Title
  371.9260941

ISBN 1-85346-132-6

Designed by Almac Ltd, London
Typeset by Cambridge Education Centre Reprographics Department
Printed in Great Britain by Bell and Bain Ltd., Glasgow

Contents

Acknowledgements

This book would not have been written without the help and support of a 'critical friend' who patiently listened, read and gave feedback whilst it was being put together. Similarly the book could not have happened without those assistants who, both formally and informally, gave me insights into their working lives. The contribution of those colleagues who field tested the pilot materials and gave critical feedback on them, has also been invaluable. Appreciation is also due to the tutor who supported me throughout my M.A. research, which led to the writing of this book. Finally, but not last in importance, I must mention Sue, who painstakingly typed on her desk top publishing system, transforming my scribble to legibility and reality. To all - 'Thank you!'

My 'critical friend' says - 'You learn much more by writing a book than reading one' - and having done it I couldn't agree more! However, I hope that my learning will benefit readers, their schools and, in particular, their assistants.

M. H. Balshaw
Cambridge, May, 1991

Introduction

The aim of this book is to help schools make better use of classroom assistants. It begins by examining the work of classroom assistants employed to work with pupils said to have special educational needs in mainstream schools. It outlines major issues with regard to their deployment, support and training. A key feature of this is the need for their training to be sited in school in order for it to be relevant, i.e. meeting the contextual needs of the assistants, as they work as part of the school's overall provision to meet the needs of children.

The book goes on to explain why this school-sited staff development is most likely to be effective if it is seen as an aspect of school development. It endorses the notion of supporting change in schools through staff development. The key proposal, therefore, is that in order to take account of the ways in which adults learn best, collaborative inquiry should be the strategy used. Collaborative inquiry involves all adults exploring their working practice together on equal footing, and agreeing goals for development.

It is recommended that this inquiry can take place at two levels. One is to examine and develop practice within existing school policy - the other is a more fundamental consideration and review of how both school practice and school policy might develop. This review is based on a series of principles developed as a result of research into the assistants' working lives. The materials offered in Part 2 of the book are practical guidelines to develop the inquiry process.

The book offers a radical stance with regard to assistants working in the field of special educational needs in that it does *not* provide the more traditional range of tips and skills for staff working with children who are perceived to have difficulties.

The first part of the book offers the background and rationale for the practical materials which form the second part. The readership for the first part is anybody who is interested in the reasoning behind the materials. It is *essential* reading for members of the school staff who may choose to co-ordinate some work in the school based on the materials in Part 2. Of particular importance is Chapter 4, which offers comprehensive instructions and support to the co-ordinator of any work i.e. 'organising collaborative inquiry'.

Part 1

CONTEXT AND RATIONALE

CHAPTER 1

Examining the Work
of Classroom Assistants

This first chapter explains the reasons that led to the writing of this book. It tells what prompted my interest and inquiry into the working lives of assistants. There is an explanation of how assistants have become such a significant part of the provision for special educational needs over the last ten years. There follows a brief description of the results of an inquiry I carried out, drawing out the significant issues as I see them with regard to assistants' social and working contexts and conditions.

The analogy is drawn between tensions and struggles at a basic conceptual level which the whole education system is experiencing, and the kinds of tensions experienced by the assistants with whom I have worked. An explanation of what might be done about this, and a suggestion for some actions that schools might take in order to resolve some of the difficulties I have found, are also offered. Of particular significance is the issue of where and how assistants are best trained in order to meet their needs and the needs of the schools in which they work.

What created the initial interest and inquiry?

I first became interested in learning support or special needs assistants and their work as long ago as 1986. This was when I was newly appointed to a job as co-ordinator for special educational needs. Amongst my accountabilities was that of jointly planning, co-ordinating and presenting in-service training (INSET) for assistants working in mainstream schools. I also met assistants in schools when working there in a professional direction and support capacity; this with both teaching staff and assistants.

Meeting assistants in both their school situations and through their INSET courses made me realise the complexity of the situations in which they find themselves. The wide ranging nature of their work, the ways in which they are expected to function, and the complex nature of their management and support all became apparent to me. As co-ordinator for special educational needs I also had a brief to monitor both the success and effectiveness of the INSET courses, and also assistants' management, deployment and support in schools.

I was particularly struck by the avid way in which those assistants fortunate enough to secure a place on the INSET courses lapped up the opportunity to learn, develop confidence and skills, and perhaps more importantly, chew over their situations and problems with each other. The floodgates opened when assistants compared notes with each other about relative experiences in schools. This happened when they did it formally, with a particular focus, and informally, in conversation. It gave assistants the opportunity to offer each other and me some very explicit observations. These were about their roles, people's attitudes towards them and their feelings about all this. Here are just three examples, which provide the reader with a flavour of some of the issues they raised.

'I wanted to go to a meeting after school when AB (an officer of the LEA) was to talk about special needs and everything, and I was told it was nothing to do with me, it was for teachers.'
(A particularly ironical situation, since the officer mentioned holds the budget that funds the assistant's allocation to the school!)

'I was talking to a parent the other day and she said "Oh, you're the general dogsbody!". I had to explain what I did, I was very upset about this'
(One wonders why the parent didn't know the reasons for the assistant's presence.)

'The other thing is, when you have lessons and they've got cover like I had on Friday last week. We had a French lesson, the member of staff taking over had no idea about French, the children had got work to do, so you know - who goes round to help them? I do! And you know, I don't mind, but I think "Well, the teaching staff are getting five times the amount of money I'm getting!"'
(She definitely has a point!)

I was so struck by some of these situations and comments, that it seemed crucial to me that all these experiences and feelings should be harnessed in a form that might help to analyse them and recommend some form of action.

This led me to carry out an inquiry into the working lives of these assistants. This book is the culmination of much of the analysis, thinking and writing carried out during that inquiry.

Why are there so many assistants in mainstream schools?

In England and Wales the catalyst which brought this about was undoubtedly the Warnock Report of 1978. This was followed by Government responses; first a White Paper and then the 1981 Education Act. As a result, Local Education Authorities (LEAs) increased and changed their range of provision for children with special educational needs in response to the new thinking espoused by Warnock and endorsed by the 1981 Act.

Briefly, this new thinking is that children with difficulties or disabilities of varying complexity should, as far as possible, be educated in their own local schools. This fits in with the philosophy of meeting their individual needs by

Help in the classroom

giving them access to a full range of curriculum experiences with their peers, rather than segregating them from their local school community and society in general. This segregation came about as a result of placing children in categories in order that they could be provided with appropriate care given by specialist teachers. The shift of emphasis from categories, care and segregation to needs, curriculum and integration is well documented in the literature by Ainscow and Muncey (1989), Ainscow (1989), Booth *et al* .(1987), Fulcher (1989), Goacher *et al.* (1988) and Norwich (1990).

Another change that has come about is that it is recognised that a much larger number of children may well experience difficulties of some kind at some time in their school lives (often temporarily). By definition this means that large numbers of teachers (if not all) share responsibility for the teaching of a much wider range of children. [Accommodation of this diversity, particularly in mainstream schools, has come to be seen as a need which creates a demand for extra forms of adult support.]

[LEAs began to employ gradually larger and larger numbers of non-teaching, and in the main, non-qualified assistants to work in mainstream schools as part of a range of provision on offer to meet special educational needs after the 1981 Act. It was seen as a positive step forward in meeting the needs of the individual children and their schools. The assistants are generally seen as working with either specified individuals or groups of children with special educational needs. They are employed on a variety of contracts, often temporary and part-time, which are reviewed at varying intervals, depending on the needs of the child(ren). Very few have formal qualifications for the role on taking up post, and most LEAs appear not to require or expect any. For an interesting overview of some of these issues Clayton (1990) is a useful resource.]

A whole range of terminology has now developed in describing the assistants. Amongst these are special support assistants, welfare assistants, support ancillaries, special needs assistants, learning support assistants (and in the United States of America and Canada 'paraprofessionals').

[A recent survey indicates that only 26 LEAs in this country have to date provided any systematic in-service training or induction training for their mainstream assistants (Goacher *et al.* 1988).] The LEA in which I work however, is at the forefront of developments in in-service training opportunities. It has mainly employed assistants with no formal qualifications, but recognised the need for INSET planned to meet the assistants' needs arising within their roles. A programme of introductory (Level 1) courses and Level 2 modules had been devised, the first of which was in 1985. Broadly these courses were seen as developing assistants' skills in working with children with special educational needs, but some have emphasised the need to work co-operatively with other adults. It was partly through working with assistants in evaluating the effectiveness of these courses that caused me to make an inquiry into their roles, support and INSET needs.

What are the experiences of assistants working in mainstream contexts?

In exploring the contexts in which assistants work and examining their roles and working lives I focused on three questions:

- What do assistants actually do?
- What are their INSET/staff development needs?
- What are the perceptions, attitudes and feelings surrounding them and their roles?

What do assistants actually do?

What assistants actually do is a very complex issue. I never cease to be impressed by the range of duties they undertake, nor the apparently wide gulf between what their job descriptions (if they have them) suggest and what they actually do.

I found that what they do falls into five broad categories of support:

- *educational*, consisting very much of supporting the curriculum approaches being used;
- *pastoral*, including the support of the children's social and behavioural well-being;
- *liaison*, involving making contact with various members of staff in the school with regards to preparation or organisation;
- *ancillary*, including basic tasks such as photocopying resources or preparing books;
- *physical*, mainly supporting youngsters with physical disabilities or difficulties.

The assistants appear to engage in tasks falling mostly into the first three categories - educational, pastoral and liaison support, with the third - liaison, being particularly common in secondary schools. Working in ancillary support is more common in nursery and primary schools. Physical support is less common as this tends to be working closely with the relatively small proportion of children with physical disabilities rather than the larger numbers of children perceived to have learning and behavioural difficulties.

When I ask assistants what their accountabilities are, many have never seen a written job description, or been party to agreeing what they should do. A majority have not seen any policy document (such as LEA guidelines for assistants). Their preparation for daily or weekly responsibilities appears to often occur incidentally ("on the hoof" as one put it). Opportunities for reviewing their work seem to be few and far between. They often use their 'common sense' or initiative in situations, in the absence of any real direction. There also appear to be many instances of teachers not being prepared for them to be in their lessons. In particular, lessons may not be organised to make effective use of this extra resource. More generally at the level of managing the role, the teachers face difficulties over how and when to do this.

However, having said all of the above things, and acknowledging that they are somewhat negative in tone, I have found examples of assistants who are comfortable with their role, know what they are expected to do and feel there is adequate support for them. In such instances they are included in planning sessions, and are regarded positively as part of the school's general provision for special educational needs. I shall go on to examine some of the factors leading to these differing experiences in school later in this chapter and in Chapter 2.

What are the assistants' INSET needs?

The following areas are those which help to focus on what assistants need. In looking at the INSET opportunities open to them and their comments and opinions about these, (and remembering that recent surveys suggest that very few LEAs do provide forms of INSET), I reached these conclusions:

- that courses offered by LEAs provide a valuable opportunity to meet other assistants (particularly those who are 'isolated' due to being the only one in school);
- that courses do give confidence and impart skills;
- that they fail to 'please all of the people all of the time' - despite obvious gratitude that they actually happen;
- that there is a need for more emphasis on working effectively with other adults, as well as children;
- that there is resentment about doing courses in their 'own time' rather than in working hours;
- that there are certain areas of need which are so 'context-specific' that centrally determined assistants' courses cannot hope to meet those needs;
- that there is a need for some practical and concrete help for schools in order that they can develop their own responses to the INSET needs of assistants.

I shall later go on to examine the last two items above in detail. They underpin my arguments for the siting of staff development for assistants in school, alongside other members of the staff. They also form the basis of the practical materials in Part 2 of this book. The evidence points to the necessity to meet assistants' needs for support as identified in the context of the social processes of the school. Therefore staff development *in situ* focusing on these contextual issues is essential. There will be further amplification of this key issue in the next chapter.

What are the perceptions, attitudes and feelings surrounding assistants and their roles?

Assistants' descriptions of people's perceptions about them and their role, the resultant attitudes shown and how they felt about these were of great interest and showed sensitivity to the situations in which they found themselves.

In looking at the assistants' comments and my analysis of their working contexts and experiences it seems that many of the difficulties expressed reflect the ethos and culture of the school in which the assistants work. How the staff and other adults deal with policy, practice and provision for special educational needs is a major influence. As part of these provisions and resources, assistants are an inseparable aspect of this central issue.

Perceptions, attitudes and resulting feelings with regard to assistants often mirror perceptions and attitudes towards the topic of special educational needs. Where assistants were positive about their roles, responsibilities and relationships there tended to be a clearer idea of the direction the whole school was taking. Where perceptions of, and attitudes to, assistants were negative or confused then it seemed that the school in general was confused about its overall policy, practice and provision.

I also found some examples of assistants being positive about their working conditions, and these more positive aspects help to inform the debate about underlying causes. These underlying causes have helped me to identify six areas which are worth examining in some detail. These areas of principle form the major planks of my arguments about how schools might well go about reviewing and developing their practice with regard to assistants specifically, and probably widen that process in order to consider their perceptions, policy, practice and provision for meeting the needs of all children.

What are the causes of the tensions found?

I now intend to examine the underlying causes of some of the difficulties and tensions experienced by the assistants, described in the previous sections of this chapter. In order to do this it is necessary to revisit the concept of special educational needs and explore the evolving policy and changing provision since Warnock.

Traditional assumptions about policy and provision were built upon the idea that special educational needs were the products of difficulties and disabilities in children. This has become commonly known as the 'child-deficit' model. Newer assumptions espouse the notion of difficulties being caused by a mismatch between what pupils are asked to do, the way in which they are asked to do it, and what they can do. This has come to be known as the 'interactive' model. Further reading about these changing trends can be found in Ainscow (1989), Ainscow and Tweddle (1988), Barton (1988) and Tomlinson (1982).

LEAs, schools and individuals have been making differing attempts to move from the first position to the second. However, this process of change is, or can be, a painful one which I would characterise as a 'struggle'. This 'struggle' is not between people, although sometimes it does become so, but about people struggling to come to terms with the process of change. LEAs, schools and individuals have difficulty in adjusting to the necessity of altering their perceptions, policy, practice and provision. There are many underlying reasons for this, but deep-rooted assumptions and attitudes, coupled with a reliance on previous practice, which often feels organisationally comfortable, are two of the major ones. Resourcing issues, which are a major influence on policy and practice, particularly in LEAs, but also in schools, often hinge on a reliance upon the bureaucratic neatness of the old model. This 'neatness' is to do with categories of children, who appeared to fit neatly into forms of provision which are determined by the children's difficulties.

The reluctance to move away from bureaucratic procedures which seemed to work in the past, despite good intentions to do so, is a crucial area of tension. There is often a rhetoric-reality gap here. Many managers and organisers 'believe' in the assumptions behind the need to consider curriculum areas. An agreement to avoid creating special educational needs through the examination of curriculum development and access is often made philosophically and spoken of rhetorically. However, practice still reflects a reliance on the old procedures. It is organisationally easier to deal with special educational needs if they are seen as created by children's difficulties, and resources are targeted at overcoming these 'deficits'.

This confusion, within the struggle to bring about change, has been influenced by human rights and equal opportunities issues at a much wider level, and is mirrored in the difficulties assistants can experience. As part of the provision for special needs, whose practice is often clearly not as well defined as it might be, it is possible to trace their difficulties back to the confusion in perceptions and policy within the education system generally. This is reflected in individual schools particularly as they seek to come to terms with their stances in these areas.

Many assistants have been allocated to schools on the 'child-deficit' assumption. They are seen as being there because of inherent difficulties children have, and their role is seen as compensating for these deficits in children.

However, in some schools, there is clearly a different direction in perception and policy. There is an attempt in these schools to move to the position of recognising that schools often create special needs by failing to make curricular and organisational responses to meet individual needs. Therefore, they are attempting to work in a way that examines using all resources (including assistants) effectively to support curriculum responses and develop flexible teaching approaches. Assistants in these schools are seen as part of this effective use of resources. Consequently they are deployed in imaginative ways, used flexibly as part of this range of resources, and recognised as being part of the whole team.

So what does this mean for you?

As you read this explanation of the 'struggle' in which all developed education systems are engaged at present, I expect that you will find that it resonates to a lesser or greater extent with the culture of your own school. All schools are likely to be involved in this struggle. However, some are involved in this process without realising the far reaching implications of it for their assistants.

I hope that you may have identified, in reading this, which part of the 'struggle' it is which affects your school provision for special educational needs, wherever you are along the road in leaving the old notions behind, and coming to terms with the new ones. These new perspectives can make the whole school outlook about its policy, provision and pupils' individual achievements much more positive. This must be so, in contrast to one which was based on 'the best we can do is compensate for these children's difficulties'.

The principles which I offer at the beginning of the next chapter will help schools to engage in this debate from the focus of the role and support of assistants. When schools consider this topic, it is likely that they will have to acknowledge the wider 'struggle'. The school may well have to accept a challenge to its overall perceptions and attitudes, policy and direction, practice and provision with regard to the special or individual needs of its pupils. At this point it is important that the reader understands that although the suggested work involving the support and deployment of the assistants in the school is the focus of the proposals I put forward, those using the contents of this book must be prepared for the perceptions, direction and provision in the school to be challenged and debated. This could well have far-reaching consequences, and I offer this 'author's health warning' at this point! I will expand on this issue in Chapter 2.

Help in the classroom

CHAPTER 2

Developing Policy and Practice

This chapter outlines the rationale behind the six principles upon which the materials in Part 2 of the book are based. It goes on to explain the necessity to decide on how to use them, whether at the level of reviewing practice with teaching staff and assistants who are working together, or at a review of policy and practice at whole-school level.

It is possible to consider your practice in school, whilst keeping in mind the notion of the 'struggle' I described in Chapter 1, and your school's place in this, and move forward as a result of this review. Using the six principles offered here it is possible to review your school's practice, and, if you wish to, its policy.

The materials in Part 2 of this book are presented in six units. They are intended to be used in a practical manner to create the climate for a collaborative inquiry into the school's practice and policy. It is *essential* to read the rationale behind the principles before attempting to put the materials into practice.

The headings in inverted commas which follow the principles in the list below are *actual* quotes from assistants about their perceived lot in life, and relate directly to the issues covered by that particular principle.

The six principles are:

- ROLES AND RESPONSIBILITIES - Classroom assistants should be clear about their roles and responsibilities - 'PIGGY IN THE MIDDLE'

- COMMUNICATION - Classroom assistants should understand the communication system in the school - 'NO-MAN'S-LAND'

- CONSISTENCY OF APPROACH - Classroom assistants should be seen positively as part of the provision to meet children's needs -'DOGSBODY'

- A WORKING TEAM - Classroom assistants should be part of a working team - 'SPY IN THE CLASSROOM'

- USING PERSONAL SKILLS - Classroom assistants should be encouraged to make use of their personal skills - 'OVERGROWN PUPIL'

- STAFF DEVELOPMENT NEEDS - Classroom assistants should be helped to develop their personal and professional skills alongside other members of staff - 'LEFT UP IN THE AIR'

The rationale for each of the six principles is as follows:

Roles and responsibilities

Classroom assistants should be clear about their roles and responsibilities

It is important that schools should recognise the need for assistants to have clearly defined and understood job-descriptions.

When asked about these matters some assistants give examples of spending far too much time being unclear about their roles and responsibilities. One described herself as the 'piggy in the middle', caught between the teacher and the children and unclear about how to respond. It is unlikely that an assistant feeling like this will be able to work to the best of her ability as it sounds like a recipe for confusion and difficulty, and clearly there is a need for the school to address the issue. If assistants are confused and uncertain about what they should be doing and why, then they may well feel that much of their time and effort is not being used to the best advantage.

There are also examples of assistants who are sure of their role in the school, and are working efficiently as a result. So some schools are definitely able to sort out these areas of potential difficulty for their assistants. Here is an example that you might like to consider:

> 'What we do, we discuss at the end of term and the beginning of the year and get our rota of how we're going to work, and then discuss it with the class teacher - we have meetings every day'.

Where assistants are as positive as the one above then it is likely that the school is clear on its policy in this area, and this is reflected in sound practice. Achieving this level of sound practice requires reviewing the practice concerning the roles and responsibilities of the assistants. It makes sense to do this. Not only must a clear definition of the role be set out to begin with, but a system of checking how well it is working in each situation/classroom is necessary. This is a whole school issue, in so far as assistants are seen as a whole school resource, and anyone who is involved in working directly with assistants should be regularly reviewing their practice.

An assistant's description of a recent development helps to make these issues 'come alive':

> 'Last week we had a meeting involving the assistants and the teachers
> who work with them, it was timetabled, the deputy head helped over
> cover, and everybody agreed to manage without their assistants for the
> last part of the afternoon. We reviewed all the links we had made across
> the school, where it was working well, where it wasn't. We had a good
> think about *why*, tried to pinpoint the way difficulties arose. It was ever so
> useful, and everybody will now have an individual meeting to discuss with
> the teacher they work most with, to review their job descriptions, and how
> the daily routine fits into them, and write something down, so we can
> review it together at the end of term. I've been feeling so positive since
> then, it's great to work and plan with the teachers about what we do. I'm a
> lot happier now!'

It is important to note that not only is she feeling a lot happier, clearer about what
she is supposed to do, she is probably working much more effectively as a result.

In most schools where there are assistants, quite a number of teaching staff
have sessions where they have assistants working with them. Consequently it is
important to review the working practice around the roles in each case.

The roles cannot be regarded as static. If the aim for the role is to encourage
all pupils to become independent learners, then the changing needs of the pupils
will call for changes in the role, and a flexibility in its uses.

Schools which neglect the need for reviewing and monitoring assistants' roles
will find that assistants may become less effective in the work they are doing,
through no fault of their own, but because the 'system' is letting them down.
They can then become increasingly dispirited, and lose their way, knowing they
could be put to better use, even if they are not quite so sure how!

The job will only develop into a productive one, and therefore provide a well-
used resource for the school, if it is viewed flexibly. In this way it can help to meet
the needs of the pupils, the teachers, the curriculum *and* the assistants!

Communication

*Classroom assistants should understand the communication system of the
school*

It is important to make sure that assistants are drawn into the communication
system of the school. This is of particular importance when assistants work part-
time. Assistants need to know what is happening, or they may find themselves
in what one described to me as 'no-man's-land'. Basic information such as who
is visiting the school this week, who is leaving at the end of term, or changes in
duty rotas can easily be 'lost' to assistants unless positive steps are taken to draw
them into the information system in the school.

Attendance at staff meetings during their contracted hours is one way in
which this can be ensured. Participation in section/departmental meetings held

for organisation and planning purposes is also advisable. Making sure that all staff who will be receiving assistant support, know about this and are able to plan for it seems a basic point, but it is surprising how often it doesn't happen. Here is an example:

> 'Even now, I go into a class and I have no idea what the lesson is going to be about. How can I get anything ready if I've had no response from the teacher?'

Clearly here there was a breakdown of communication, or possibly even an absence of any intention to communicate. This pinpoints the necessity for reliable systems of communication, of which the assistant is part.

It may be necessary to review the school practice with regards to communication with *and* about the assistants working there. Not only do assistants need to be aware of what is going on (at all kinds of levels), but other people need to know about them - why they are there, what they do, and how they fit in.

An assistant's description of an incident that happened to her illustrates the need for this to be considered, and the crucial question of 'who' should know 'what' comes to the fore.

> 'The other thing is, when you have lessons and they've got cover, like I had on Friday last week. We had French, the member of staff had *no* idea about French, the children had got work to do, so you know, who goes round to help them? I do! and you know, I don't mind, but I think *"Well,* the teaching staff are getting *five times* the amount of money I'm getting!"'

Amongst people who need to know about assistants, who they are, and what they do, are the school staff who do not regularly or presently have assistant support in the normal timetable, and supply teachers, internal and external. Parents, who should also know, may ask why they are there, as should governors and other professionals such as speech therapists and physiotherapists. You will probably be able to think of others to whom this would apply who either work in or visit your school.

Consistency of approach

Classroom assistants should be seen positively as part of the provision to meet children's needs

It is important that assistants should be employed in a consistent and productive manner in the school. They should not experience the feeling of being a 'general dogsbody' - which is the way at least one assistant has described herself.

It is particularly difficult if assistants find enormous differences between teachers in the way they are expected to work. Of course, working practice *is* almost bound to vary to some degree, because of differing personalities and teaching styles. However, there should be an agreed set of 'groundrules'. This takes you back to the importance of a job description and its 'interpretation' by various teachers. A teacher explains some of the issues:

"We're clear about who's doing what before we start, because we've worked out a pattern for different situations, depending on what I'm teaching. I've also talked to Mrs P about it, so when the assistant goes into her lessons on Tuesdays and Fridays she finds a similar pattern of working, but does quite different things with the children. With me she does work on topics and cross-curricular themes. Mrs P has her working on more basic curriculum areas, language and maths for example.'

A flexibility in what is done in certain aspects is obvious here, but the main 'groundrules' appear to be clear to all. This must mean that the assistant is able to be more effective, as she is being asked to work in a consistent way. It is well worth considering drawing up a set of 'groundrules' to help to create consistency throughout the school. However these will probably only go part of the way towards reducing inconsistency.

Underlying deep-rooted inconsistencies in using assistants as a resource, are uncertainties felt by individuals about what the job is about, at a much more fundamental level. A whole school policy worked out by the school is the key to reducing these uncertainties.

Attitudes and perceptions can make or break school policy. The vision and purpose in the school about its approaches to special educational needs should be clear and agreed by all the people working in and for the school. Underlying attitudes about special educational needs can create a great deal of inconsistency in both policy and practice, and this will inevitably have an impact on the working lives of the assistants. If assistants are seen as a positive part of the range of provision to meet children's needs, they will be less likely to experience the situation described here:

'The English teacher I've worked with has been very helpful, she has been very nice as a person, because some of the staff won't accept me for what we are - if they could be 100 per cent honest, don't want us in the classroom.'

It is important to recognise that such differing attitudes and stances about provision to meet children's needs, including assistants, often do exist in schools. These should be acknowledged and accounted for in considering how the assistants should work. If they are viewed positively as part of the provision then they are unlikely to experience great inconsistencies in approach to them and their work.

Reviewing the school's policy with regard to special educational needs, and drawing out within this individuals' thoughts about special educational needs and how they arise, is a positive way of opening up the debate. This process may uncover some of the reasons for inconsistency in approaches. It is also possible that having done this there may be more basis for agreement about policy and approaches, and therefore a better chance of consistency of approach.

A working team

Classroom assistants should be part of a working team

The experience of being kept at a distance, 'on the margins', is not conducive to a positive working atmosphere and good working relationships. It has even occasioned the response 'I feel like a spy in the classroom'. It seems impossible to imagine informed, constructive classroom observation using the adults in a positive collaborative way given this situation.

An involvement in planning the programme for joint working, teacher/ assistant and assistant/pupil, is essential if effort and resources are to pay off. This planning should be seen as an investment, done in working time, and not as a 'bolt-on' nuisance, even a luxury. It should be carried out in such a way as to value everybody's contribution. When this is the norm in a school then the following comment is likely:

> 'We work as a team very much, and I am allowed a lot of freedom, which I must say I do like. I like to be able to feel I'm actually thinking for myself, albeit I can always talk it over with the teachers.'

This assistant obviously feels she is very much part of a team. It seems very positive, indicating trust in the assistant to use her skills, but offering support when she needs it. Giving the assistants the opportunity to be part of the team, involved in information sharing and planning, with their contributions given value and status is a very positive step.

There may well be a need to review the school's practice with regard to how it involves assistant(s) in the whole school team. Overall membership of the wider school team is a positive step much as creating a feeling of 'belonging' to a particular working group (often a partnership). Involvement in information sharing, decision making and planning is a way of fostering this team membership at a whole school level, particularly if it takes place inside assistants' contracted hours.

Attitudinal stances with regard to the value of the assistant's contributions may well get in the way of this. These include professionalism ("they're not qualified and we are"), and perceptions of status and hierarchy, which can pose a very real difficulty in team development.

Part of being in effective teams, and indeed the way they develop, is by being listened to and having one's opinion valued. "Spies in the classroom" as an assistant was heard to say, do not tend to feel valued for their contribution to the whole! Much more positive is the following description, offered by an assistant about being in an effective team:

> 'We've been working at objectives or targets for each of us for the lessons and learning how is the best way to review that. At staff meetings the successes and failures have been talked about and we've drawn up some helpful guidelines for anybody to use. It's really good, and one of *my* ideas is in there!'

An assistant feeling positive about her contribution to team development must be a positive advantage to the work of the school, thus enhancing the learning environment provided for all the children.

Using Personal Skills

Classroom assistants should be encouraged to make use of their personal skills

It is advisable that schools attempt to make sure that people's strengths and skills are used positively, in a way that enhances the learning environment. Wasted talent amongst the adults working in the school is unfortunate and limits the overall range of responses available to meet children's needs. An assistant who feels like an 'overgrown pupil' is hardly in a helpful situation, and this is unlikely to lead to a productive use of talents. An exploration of what everybody is able to offer to a situation (within the team development and planning meetings) is likely to pay off in extending broad and balanced curriculum approaches to pupils.

A supportive relationship, fostered in the team development meetings also allows for 'weaknesses' or worries to be acknowledged, accounted for and supported.

An assistant offers here what she sees as an important contribution she would have been able to make, if somebody had asked her:

> 'I feel that because I've got children of my own, who've just been through *that* stage, I could help with suggesting ideas. The school they're at did some really interesting things which Lucy responded to very positively. I could see those two we've been having difficulty with recently would have been enthusiastic about a different approach, you know, they'd be much less bored.'

A discussion where different ideas were asked for and considered, would no doubt have helped a sensible suggestion to be brought forward, and possibly used within a range of approaches, in this situation. A word of caution however - one assistant explained that she felt the discovery of her 'talent' - which was undoubtedly genuine, had condemned her to 'overkill' on the sewing groups, to such an extent that as a 'keen seamstress' her keenness had somewhat had the edge removed!

However, there is much to be said for discovering what people are good at and using this in sensible proportions, to extend the range of opportunities available to children.

The issue of capitalising on the talents of all members of the school, including assistants, to enhance the learning environment for its pupils, begs the question - how do we establish what talents are available in a way which is sensitive and realistic? Assistants who feel like 'overgrown pupils' obviously have not had the chance to explore these issues, and are unlikely to feel that they are able to offer

B

much to the overall resources the school has to offer its pupils.

However, an assistant who is encouraged, with others in the team, to explore the way in which the talents and skills available can be used *and* developed is likely to become confident, and able to try new ideas to build on.

> 'I have quite a lot of ideas about how to work in the next bit of the National Curriculum, especially where I could bring some things we've collected at home... the trouble is, we aren't asked to contribute in that kind of way. I don't want to sit in a corner with one or two children with worksheets, it's so boring. I find it boring, so I'm sure they do!'

This assistant is clearly itching to have a go at doing something more adventurous and less boring. It is unfortunate that the school has not realised what a wasted resource they appear to have.

An exploration of the range of resources, of the human kind, taking account of the skills, opinions, likes and dislikes of all the staff, including assistants, is a positive step for the school in its quest to meet the needs of all children.

Staff development needs

Classroom assistants should be helped to develop their personal and professional needs alongside other members of staff

It is helpful to consider ways of developing the immediate group of staff in which the assistant works in order to create an atmosphere in which all the team are able to learn together. The team spends much of its time working in classrooms and effective in-service training can and does take place in these contexts, given the right atmosphere, and the recognition of the need for it.

Assistants and teachers can develop new skills and practice together through examining their working day - or part of it! This can be done in a constructively critical way, trying out new ideas and approaches together and learning as a result. They may well benefit from this approach as may the children.

Assistants who are 'left up in the air', feeling they have identified a need for some in-service training are unlikely to work as positively as those who have had a need identified *and* supported, through either school-based work or external courses. An assistant experiencing the following situation would probably consider herself to have been 'left up in the air':

> 'It was useful, that last course, but there are things it doesn't help, about how we work in school. It's all very well doing some of the things we did on the course back in school. I've tried some and they've been really useful. What it doesn't do though, is get under the skin of what happens to me in school - in the last week we were talking about somebody who had been to several staff or team meetings because they wanted her to be in on the curriculum things they were doing. I can't imagine that happening

Help in the classroom

here unless things change...'

An exploration of how the needs of assistants like this one are identified and could be met in school is an important step forward in supporting the professional development of assistants. There is much to be gained from also exploring ways in which the staff team of teachers *and* assistants might learn together.

Schools have a responsibility to ensure all staff receive appropriate staff development opportunities. Indeed they now have budgets that should support 'in-house' staff training. As a result of this policy, most of the required INSET can be experienced in schools, through the staff development plan. Assistants who have recognised a need for further training should not be left condemned to feel 'left up in the air' if their needs are acknowledged in the overall scheme of things in the school. An assistant here explains the benefit she has gained from school based INSET:

> 'I've been on two of these professional development days now. The last was about the different ways children learn - it was really interesting. It was originally to do with study skills for GCSE, but everybody decided to think about it for other things. It was very useful. Now, the teacher I work with most and I have been trying out some ideas, when we're working together - trying to make sure everybody's getting access to National Curriculum English by thinking about how they learn best.'

Support to pursue outside sources of INSET should be offered if it is impossible to meet the needs of the assistant within the school. This should also be support in *working* hours, not the assistant's free time. This kind of support can be identified in the school staff development plan in addition to those opportunities the school provides 'in-house' for all staff to learn together.

Conclusion

In presenting these six principles there are two areas which need additional explanation. One is the interlinked nature of the issues addressed by the six principles and therefore of the activities suggested in the materials in Part 2. In some ways I have put in arbitrary divisions to streamline the process. The issues in all six areas are so interwoven and interdependent that these arbitrary divisions appear to cut through these threads. You will find that as you use the materials you will, of necessity, consider some of the issues which seem to belong some where else. This is very understandable and quite acceptable, and it will in fact help you to realise that the assistants' work is a reflection of these complex, interwoven policy issues. It is not easy to divide them into 'neat' compartments. However, at a pragmatic level, in order to work at the issues systematically you should find it helpful to have these divisions. The materials will feel more controllable to you, in both their use and scope.

The second issue meriting further explanation is that of the scope and the level at which the materials might be used in your school. The question for consideration is: *how far reaching do you want these activities and implicit challenges to practice, and, more fundamentally to policy, to be?* This is a decision for whoever is responsible for co-ordinating any development using these materials with assistants and teachers in the school to take in collaboration with colleagues.

The materials can in fact be used at two levels. These are:

1) involving a consideration of how practice might be developed within existing school policy,
2) involving a consideration of how both practice *and* school policy might be developed.

You need to be aware that starting the process at Level 1 is quite likely at some stage to lead to Level 2. The question at this point therefore has to be: can we handle this, as individuals, as a team, and as a school?

At Level 1 the issue is about doing whatever you already do, better, within existing policy (i.e. 'doing things right'). Level 2 on the other hand is about attempting to 'do the right thing' in terms of new assumptions about special educational needs. That is not to say that the materials attempt to prescribe a policy for any individual school; it would be insensitive to assume that it is possible for an outsider, such as this particular author, to do that. The policy of the school *could* reflect the new assumptions in a way that meets the needs of the school. It should be devised by the personnel in the school. If your school is ready to consider its vision and purpose with regards to its policy and provision for individual children, and the assistants' role within that, then the materials in this book are aimed much more at that target.

However, I refer back here to my argument in Chapter 1. This is that if schools continue to see assistants as a reflection of the child-deficit model, therefore operating in such a way as to attempt to compensate for difficulties and disabilities in children themselves, then it *is* possible to improve that form of practice. Using some or all of the materials could well attempt to do that, within the boundaries of existing policy. This book recognises the dilemma of 'struggle' between traditional assumptions and new assumptions. Most schools are caught in a mixture of the practice of the traditional and the rhetoric of the new, and this author cannot attempt to guess at where your school is with regard to this complex issue.

'Doing the right thing' is the decision that the co-ordinator of these proposed developments would have to make, in collaboration with colleagues. I leave that with you at this point. Reviewing the situation in school is one way of coming to that decision, and in the next chapter I will put forward my rationale for carrying out that review effectively, involving all the relevant people, and making decisions about what actions to take as a result of it.

CHAPTER 3

Supporting Change Through Staff Development

This chapter is based on a set of assumptions, which are outlined. It also focuses on the needs of adults as learners. Meeting these needs is more likely to be successful at in-school level, and an explanation for this is offered through the idea of collaborative inquiry. The need to link these individual needs to school development is also outlined. This is followed by an explanation of how to carry out a process of review and development, and offers some of the theory behind what is effective practice in this field.

I start from a set of basic assumptions, and will then illustrate these in more detail, by incorporating them into my recommendations to carry out 'collaborative inquiry' into the school's practice. These assumptions are drawn from my own experiences over a number of years in attempting to provide effective staff development opportunities for a range of staff. They are also drawn from various sources in the extensive literature about staff development. These assumptions are as follows:

- The notion of staff development as a way of bringing about development and change.
- The inclusion of all the relevant people in the 'collaborative inquiry' into their practice.
- The use of a form of 'collaborative inquiry' to bring about a review of need and a plan of action.
- The expectation of a contribution to the process from all members of staff, no matter where they exist on the hierarchy.
- The principle that all individual contributions are valued as worthwhile to the whole, so that people are resources to one another.
- The development of a collegiality which celebrates individual ideas and contributions, whilst helping the team to move forward productively.

Educational Change and Development

The experience of bringing about educational change and development is well documented in the literature. Probably the most well known proponent of what effective change looks like is Michael Fullan. He states that for change to happen at all effectively it is important to involve those who will be bringing about the change in planning for it. This increases the chance of them understanding *why* the change is needed, and *how* it should be brought about. If people are to understand the need for, and the process of change, then they need to 'make sense of it as a personal process'.

Fullan also recommends that staff development is one of the ways in which the process of change can be supported. Reviewing practice, identification of areas for development, and collaborative planning about how to go about it, are all components of staff development. He also refers to the notion of adults as learners, and states that the adults (staff) who learn and therefore develop at a professional level within a collaborative environment are in a better position to carry out some effective developments. They will fare better than those who are expected to learn because somebody else decides on the need for change (plans the change), and then tells them to do it (and not always how) (Fullan, 1982; 1990; 1991).

It is worth mentioning at this point that my previous recommendation about siting staff development in schools in order to improve the work of assistants is confirmed by Fullan and his colleagues in this field. The idea that the adults, teachers and assistants, should learn together in the context which creates their staff development needs is linked to, and grows out of policies for overall staff development.

Smith (1983) outlines some principles for adults as learners, which do not only apply to teachers but any adults seeking to develop their thinking and practice. He argues that adults learn best when:

- They feel the need to learn and have input into what, why and how they will learn.
- The content and processes of learning bear a perceived and meaningful relationship to past experience, and experience is effectively utilised as a resource for learning.
- What is to be learned relates optimally to the individual's developmental changes and life tasks.
- The amount of autonomy exercised by the learner is congruent with that required by the mode or method utilised.
- They learn in a climate that minimises anxiety and encourages freedom to experiment.
- Their learning styles are taken into account.

Keeping these points in mind I recommend a form of staff development which creates conditions that will facilitate adult learning. I will call this approach 'collaborative inquiry' following the ideas of Reason (1988) who describes it as a 'holistic learning process'. The way in which this approach involves staff in a given context developing personally and professionally as part of a team which reviews its practice regularly in a collaborative learning process, allows the above conditions to exist. Using collaborative inquiry means that all of those involved (and in the case of this book, that includes assistants) are learners together about their work. This means starting with perceptions, attitudes and philosophy, going on to address reviewing and planning, strategies and action, and using inbuilt procedures for monitoring and evaluating what they are doing together. As Reason states

> 'the difference between inquiry, learning and action in the world become indistinct and unimportant, as we consider collaborative inquiry as a holistic learning process'.

The emphasis on collaboration as a means of supporting change is promoted by Thousand and Villa (1991) who have recently been involved in work in schools in the USA to support them in developing overall responses to *all* children in the local community. Their aim is that schools accommodate the widest range of student diversity possible. In doing this they have evolved 'collaborative learning processes'. They state that the power of this approach lies

> 'in the capacity to merge the unique skills of talented adults and students, enfranchise team members through the participatory decision making process, and distribute leadership authority beyond the administration to the broader school community'.

They have been guided in this by the advice offered by Johnson and Johnson (1989) about co-operative group learning (equally applicable with adults or pupils). This approach involves

- frequent face to face intervention - discussion between participants about the process of learning
- an 'all for one, one for all' feeling of positive interdependence
- a focus on the development of small group interpersonal skills
- regular assessment of team functioning
- methods for holding one another accountable for agreed upon commitments.

As Thousand and Villa state - this leads to a 'climate of equality and equity'. This surely must be a positive way to move towards valuing all contributions to the decision making process, regardless of hierarchy.

This collaborative approach also provides support systems for those involved. The process can be challenging, but the collaborative learning described involves the existence of the mutual support derived from working in the team. It is particularly important that this support exists when the work involves dealing with potential conflict. I refer here to the 'health warning' I offered before, and will conclude this section of the Chapter with some further thoughts on that subject.

Reviewing Practice and Moving into Action

Needs identification, whether for staff development or school development, is best done through a process of review of current practice. However, the process does not begin and end with review, but is cyclical in nature.

Hopkins (1989) explains that effective school and staff development are inextricably interlinked and that there is a cyclical process in which staff in schools should engage. This endorses Fullan's views about staff development and change. Examples of this type of review are GRIDS and IMTEC (IDP). Further reading about this subject can be found in Hopkins (1987) and Bollen and Hopkins (1987). The current DES document on school development by Hargreaves *et al.* (1989) also emphasises the review procedure in getting started. However, after reviewing practice there should be a cyclical process involving planning, moving into action, reviewing and monitoring the effect of the action, and the strategies employed, and then making further plans for action.

In the materials in this book I have offered a framework for the review of practice in your school with regard to your assistant(s). This is based on the six principles outlined earlier in this chapter and can be found on page 33. It follows the advice given by various researchers and authors on carrying out review procedures and offers the staff an opportunity to put forward their opinion on the school's practice. It is designed in such a way that it is likely to be able to identify common areas of interest or need for development, whilst taking account of individual opinion. This is in accordance with both the advice of Smith (1983) and that of Fullan (1990).

Having identified an area on which some staff developmental work could be done a strategy for planning and moving into action is offered. This is 'action planning' and suggests the involved personnel should answer both individually and as part of the team a set of questions. These are to be found on page 47. A diagrammatic form, which can be filled in by the group, having agreed a course of action is also part of the materials (see page 48).

This form of action planning encourages both individual and team commitments to the decisions taken, and therefore helps to build in the 'positive interdependence' that Johnson and Johnson (1989) advise. It identifies action for others than those in the immediate group of people involved, and who may be responsible for involving these members of the wider team - heads of department, headteachers, governors, LEA officers etc. might all be identified. It also includes questions which ensure that the group or team identifies realistic timescales for action, and plots dates and times for reviewing and monitoring progress either individually or together. This then allows for the next stage to be embarked upon.

In conclusion

I now return to the issue of making a decision about how wide the scope of the proposed development will be. The co-ordinator of the development will have to be aware of the necessity for a corporate decision carried out after reviewing practice in school. The group of people involved in this first review should be encouraged to consider and to discuss the matter. The co-ordinator, having a knowledge of all the notions and assumptions about a collaborative inquiry offered here, should be in a position to facilitate this discussion.

Challenging the 'status quo' may be the outcome of the team's decision. This can be an uncomfortable and difficult process and this should be acknowledged at the outset. However, if there is a commitment to 'collaborative learning' then the mutual support on offer to all members of the team should help them through 'bad patches'. (Remember, the materials offer the option to action plan at either of two levels, after deciding the scope of the development.) It may be useful here to consider the analogy of the root and the branch. It will be possible to make changes to twigs and branches without challenging wider attitudes and assumptions in school. This in itself can benefit the immediate team and its practice. However, if the 'root' of the system remains the same, then there will be severe limitations on the ability of the school as a whole to develop its perceptions, attitudes, policy, practice and provision for meeting the individual needs of all children. This, again, is the basis of my author's 'health warning'. The process can be painful, but if acknowledged as a whole school issue the benefits can be many and positive. Including the assistants in all of this work is underlined by the rationale to the six principles which are the basis of the materials, i.e. they are part of a team involved in a 'holistic learning process'.

CHAPTER 4

Organising Collaborative Inquiry

This chapter contains advice for the co-ordinator of the work in school. It consists of instructions on the use of the materials, how to run staff development sessions, in particular carrying out a review of practice and action planning and other specific group processes.

The materials in Part 2 of this book have been extensively fieldtested in a range of schools. This experience indicated that care has to be taken in order that positive conditions can be created in order to carry out collaborative inquiry. In more detail, the contents are as follows:

1. General instructions on the use of the materials
2. Advice on how to run the sessions, including:
   - general advice
   - preparation for sessions
   - pre-session reading
   - introductions to sessions
   - group sizes
   - timings
   - ending of sessions
   - planning/negotiating further sessions
3. Instructions on how to:
   - carry out a review of practice
   - action planning
       questions to ask
       an outline
       planning - at what level?
       review of action
4. Specific instructions on:
   - Brainstorming
   - Nominal Group Technique
   - Brick Walls
5. Some final points

1. General instructions

The materials in Part 2 are intended for flexible use in any or all of the following ways:

- a series of workshops (free standing) [Level 1 and/or Level 2]

- a staff development session (e.g. on professional development, 'Baker days') for whole school [Level 1 and/or Level 2]

- as a focus for a team or departmental meeting [Level 1]

- as a series of team development meetings over a period of time to be determined by the participants [Level 1 and/or Level 2]

They can be used by one teacher and one assistant as a minimum (producing a dialogue for staff development) although most activities would require a third party as resource/observer. They can be used by the whole school staff, or by any sized group in between. Guidance is given on group sizes in each of the various activities.

It is intended that whatever the size of the group it should include *at least one assistant*. This will:

- provide support and staff development for the assistant(s)
- involve the assistants' perceptions, opinions, skills, ideas and actions, in the team/staff developments that result.

The materials should be used in the following order:

1. Review of Practice
2. Choice of Unit to be used as a result of the Review
3. Use of action planning advice as a seminar for intended participants (if appropriate)
4. Use of the relevant Unit and section of that suggested by the Review of Practice
5. Action planning and developments
6. Review of action taken.

2. Advice on how to run the sessions

General advice

In using the materials with your colleagues remember the notion of a 'collaborative inquiry'.

It is important to create a comfortable atmosphere for the sessions with appropriate accommodation and seating, but also through the 'climate' created in the group(s).

The co-ordinator should not be considered the 'fount of all knowledge'. In a collaborative inquiry everybody has something to offer which is worthwhile. You as co-ordinator are in a position to reflect back questions, drawing others in to see how they would answer the question that has been directed at you.

Having encouraged people's contributions, it is important to acknowledge them, particularly when they come from somebody who had to 'pluck up courage' to respond.

Where there are continuous negative comments from one or more people in the group then the group should be encouraged to find strategies to overcome the 'ah but's...'. It may be possible to use the 'Brick Walls' technique detailed on page 42 as a means of getting participants to think more positively about matters under consideration. This is also the main process used in Unit 3: Section 2 of the materials.

Pre-session reading

Circulating a copy of the pre-session reading to all the intended participants is important, in order for them to come to the session prepared.

This should be done early enough for people to have time to read it (two or three days, or a weekend), rather than a week or more, which often means people either will read it and forget about it, or think 'I've got plenty of time' and never get round to it!

A reminder to people the day before, to read their copies and bring them to the session can be helpful. This should be given in gentle fashion so as not to be seen as 'nagging'.

The pre-session reading is a short version of the rationale behind the six principles, given in Chapter 2, Part 1, couched in reasonably simple terms. This will prepare participants for the issues to be considered.

Preparation for the sessions

It is important to prepare the materials and the room to be used for the sessions, and to make sure the session will not be interrupted.

Adequate copies of all the materials, and other resources listed in the co-ordinator's guidelines (the first page of each Section in each Unit), should be prepared. It can be very unsettling for a group if the co-ordinator disappears in the middle of a session to photocopy frantically something forgotten, or more copies if there are not enough.

You may well find it worthwhile to conduct a short 'seminar' on the principles of action planning prior to using the Units themselves, as it is a core process activity and as such, very important. To do this, talking would-be participants through the materials in Section 3 of this chapter would be helpful.

Making sure that you feel prepared yourself for the sessions is at least as important, if not more, than preparing others, and the materials. Be sure that you are comfortable about both the content *and* process issues in which you will be engaging, and your role in these.

It is best for you to be part of the group(s), not sitting apart as if you don't belong. You will have a better insight into the issues discussed if you do this, but of course it does mean that your own preparation must be thorough, so that you can be a group member and the group facilitator simultaneously.

Introduction to the sessions

State, or re-state the aims for the session, as written in the materials.

Remind people of the main points in the pre-session reading, or give them a few moments to refresh their memories by re-scanning their copies.

If there is *any* possibility that you have people in the group who do not know one another, make sure introductions are done. This is not impossible, particularly if you are working at whole-school level in a big school.

Be clear at the start how long the session will last.

Group sizes

Details about optimum group sizes are given with each set of materials.

If people are somewhat reticent to volunteer comments into the 'big' group it is

Help in the classroom

generally better to get people to 'chat with a neighbour/partner' first of all, then perhaps talk in fours, before the whole group attempts discussion.

You will find it useful to allow for this in the suggested programme for the group activity, so that people do have the opportunity for discussion in a non-threatening way.

Timings

Timings given are advisory, and are to do as much with the *proportion* of the overall time as the length. If for any reason you have to alter the *overall* length, or split the session into two shorter sections, keep the *proportions* for the various sections of the activity similar to those suggested.

Stick to the time to finish stated and agreed at the outset, even if, as the session goes on, people are seen to be very engaged in the tasks. They may be, but still would wish to finish at the agreed time.

Ending the sessions

Where a debrief is suggested, make sure that *has* taken place. Sometimes it is worth finishing the activity itself five minutes (or so) early in order to debrief more fully, and summarise the agreed actions clearly once more.

Finish on time - don't risk alienating people.

Planning and negotiating future sessions

Guidance on this is given in both the relevant Sections of the Units and the action planning guidelines.

However, having the group together is an ideal opportunity to set dates, and much better than attempting to do it piecemeal or through memos afterwards.

3. Instructions on the Review of Practice

Each person who will be involved in using the materials should fill in the review schedule. It is particularly important that *all* assistants are encouraged to fill it in.

Using a rating scale of 1 to 5:
    1 = needs little or no improvement
    5 = there is room for substantial improvement.

The schedule should be filled in (anonymously if you wish) and handed back to the co-ordinator of the developments. It can, if preferred, be used in a discussion session.

The collated results i.e. those showing group preferences for starting in certain areas and those showing discrepancies among individuals, should be shared with those who completed the review schedules.

Where there is a clear area identified by a majority of people then the activities for that principle may then be used.

Where there is no clear area identified then further discussion should take place in order to reach agreement on an area for development, amongst the people who will be involved.

Review of practice

In which areas of our team's/department's/school's practice should we make improvements?

Based on these six statements of principle please ring the rating scale on the basis of:

    ① needs little or no improvement ——>   ⑤ needs a great deal of improvement.

Classroom assistants should:

    i)   be clear about their roles and responsibilities   1 2 3 4 5

    ii) understand the communication system in the school   1 2 3 4 5

    iii) be seen positively as part of the range of provision to meet children's needs   1 2 3 4 5

    iv) be members of a working team   1 2 3 4 5

    v)   be encouraged to make use of their personal skills   1 2 3 4 5

    vi) be helped to develop their personal and professional skills alongside other members of staff   1 2 3 4 5

Please hand in to _____

By _____

Thank you.

Moving into action

General points

The materials for Action Planning can be used flexibly to suit the school's and individual's needs.

You may find it useful to provide a seminar for the people you expect to be involved in using the materials in the Units. This seminar should take the form of a discussion about the process of action planning. The co-ordinator should guide the participants through the action planning questions and the process, encouraging questions and clarification of the process.

The rest of this part of the chapter deals with:
- questions to ask to help you to plan
- an action plan outline
- planning - at what level?
- reviewing the actions taken.

Action planning questions

As a group or individually you will find it helpful to answer the following questions in the order suggested.

WHAT   •   do you intend to do now? (short term objective)
- as individuals
- as teachers
- as assistants
- as a team?

WHY   •   do you intend to do it?
(Do NOT miss out answering this question - it is of *vital* importance!)

HOW   •   do you intend to do it?
e.g. contact/discussion/meetings/in-service sessions

WHOM • do you intend to involve in it?
i.e. just yourselves or others not here now
e.g. senior management/head/governors/parents/pupils/
INSET Co-ordinator/LEA staff

BY WHEN • do you intend to have achieved your shorter term objective?
How will you know you have?

• do you intend to have achieved your longer term objective?

WHEN • WILL YOU REVIEW AND EVALUATE?
(Who will monitor and review?)
(Who will evaluate and how?)

REMEMBER
TO • State why you propose to take the actions you are planning.

• Keep your timescale realistic.

• Put a review/evaluation procedure into place.

• Give everyone a copy of the finalised version.

Figure 4.1 Action planning outline

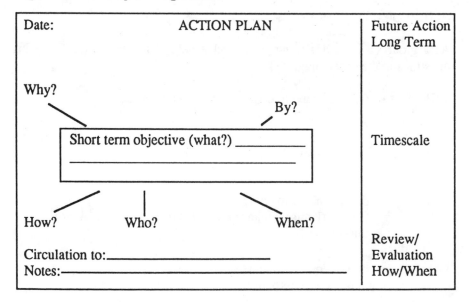

Help in the classroom

Reviewing the Action

As a group remind yourselves of your immediate objective(s) and *why* you decided on that course of action.

Each individually review your responsibility within the plan and what happened.

Consider *why* it happened.

What helped progress?

What hindered progress?

As a group consider your collaborative plan of action. What happened? Why? What helped/hindered?

Were there any 'unintended outcomes'? If so, what were they?

Do you need to re-draw the action plan?

If so, go back to the original questions:

What?
Why?
How?
Who?
When?
How/when will we monitor/evaluate?

If you do not, and are satisfied with progress and developments made, set a date to review this. Then you will need to ask:

- has progress been maintained?   How?
- are practices still improved?   In what ways?

Action Planning - at what level?

Action Planning at Level 1

Do you wish (as a group) to attempt the kinds of activities aimed at Level 1 - a review and development of practice, as suggested by your activity outlines? If YES, Then Level 1 Action Planning deals with smaller scale developments in practice within present agreed school policy. (This does not preclude working at Level 2 sometime in the future.)

OR - Action planning at Level 2

The issues you have identified as a result of your activity using the materials in Section 1 of your chosen Unit may suggest to you that Action planning on a small scale will not be sufficient. To be addressed in enough depth a review of school policy with regard to those issues may well be helpful.

The following questions might help you to draw up an interim plan to facilitate the move into Level 2 action, using the materials in Section 2 of the Unit on which you have been working:

- Do you wish to use the materials in Section 2 of this Unit? These address wider issues to do with whole-school approaches and policy.

- How will you (as a co-ordinator, or as a group) organise time and space to do it? When? How?

- Indeed, can you do so?

- Does it necessitate senior management/headteacher's backing to do it? It may well do so, as it is aimed at more fundamental issues than Level 1.

- How would you expect them to back you -
    in principle?
    at a practical level - in shape of time/resources?

- Should this proposed action go into the school development plan? If so, how will it get there?

- What about the timescale you are able to set yourselves?

- What else may compete with what you want to do?

You may also find it useful to refer to Fullan and Park's advice about whether the school is ready for this kind of action at this point; how receptive it might be to change and its implementation. Figure 4.2 is West and Ainscow's (1991) version - couched in familiar terms rather than in North American terminology, which refers to 'school systems and school boards'.

Implementation: 'the process of altering existing practice in order to achieve more effectively certain desired outcomes for pupils'.

According to Fullan and Park (1981) twelve factors seem to be especially critical. Consider these with respect to your own development plans.

Fig. 4.2 Implementing change in school

	Yes	No	Not sure
A. The nature of the change			
1. Do those involved accept the need for change?			
2. Is the proposed change understood by those involved?			
3. Are necessary resources available?			
B. Characteristics of the school system			
4. Have previous attempts at change been successful?			
5. Do the headteacher and others who will need to take a lead have support?			
6. Will there be staff development for all those involved?			
7. Is the change supported by the governors and parents?			
8. Are there plans to monitor the process of implementation over time?			
9. Are there strategies to avoid overload as a result of too many innovations during the same period?			
C. Characteristics of the school			
10. Is the headteacher prepared to take an active role in supporting the change?			
11. Will teachers provide support for one another?			
D. External factors			
12. Will there be support from external agencies?			

4. Specific Instructions

Brainstorming

This approach is useful in creating an agenda for discussion within the group. For a set period participants offer ideas or comments related to the issue under consideration.

One of the group members records the contributions, preferably onto a flipchart, blackboard or overhead projector, so all can see them.

Rules should be followed strictly by participants. This is in order that *all* participants feel confident to offer ideas without fear of criticism.

Rules:
- All ideas related to the issues in any direct way are expected.
- A maximum number of related ideas is expected.
- One idea may be modified, adapted or expressed as another idea.
- Ideas should be expressed in a clear and concise manner.
- No discussion of the ideas should be allowed or attempted.
- There should be *no* criticism of ideas.

Once the list has been gathered, by the end of the brainstorming period, the agenda for normal discussion is ready.

Nominal Group Technique

A method of obtaining group responses to questions or problems which:

- ensure that everybody contributes
- avoids the dominance of the group by a few people with strong ideas
- avoids too narrow an interpretation of the task
- ensures a wide variety of responses
- allows a systematic ordering of priorities.

The Procedure

Clarification of the Task
The task is presented on a blackboard, flipchart or overhead projector (e.g. 'How can the school's communication system be improved?'). In order that all participants fully understand the question, time is spent in group discussion about the nature of the task.

Silent nominations

Individuals are given a fixed period to list their own private responses. This should not be hurried. They are then asked to rank their own list in order to establish felt priorities.

Master list

The group leader compiles a master list on the blackboard, flipchart or overhead projector taking *only* one item from each group member in rotation. No editing of the material is allowed and no evaluating comments are to be made at this stage. It is helpful to number the items.

Item clarification

During this phase each item is discussed until all members know what it means. Clarification only is allowed. If a member of the group now feels their item is already covered by someone elses, they may request its withdrawal. No pressure should be applied to any individual to have items withdrawn or incorporated in another.

Evaluation

It is now necessary to decide the relative importance of items in the eyes of the group. Each person is allowed five weighted votes (i.e. five points for the item that is felt to be most important, four points for the next, and so on). A simple voting procedure allows the consensus to emerge.

Once the composite picture has emerged, it provides an agenda for normal group discussions to proceed.

Reminder to group leaders

- Do not reinterpret a person's ideas.

- Use the participant's own wording.

- Do not interject your own ideas - YOU ARE NOT PARTICIPATING.

- Give people time to think.

- This is *not* a debate - do not allow participants to challenge each other or attempt to persuade each other.

- Do not try to interpret results - do not look for patterns.

Brick Walls

This approach is particularly useful when considering how to implement a plan, or when considering the question 'What gets in the way of me/us reaching the desired objective?'

In pairs or small groups there is discussion to consider how the bricks in the way might be removed, by either individual or team effort. Participants may also be asked to think whether any of the 'blocks' are of their own making.

At a group level, each person may offer one of their individual 'blocks' to a 'group brick wall' with a team or group objective to achieve. Then the group can discuss strategies for removing the bricks that are in the way, by either individual or team efforts. A consideration may also be given to acknowledging that at a certain stage some of the bricks are 'beyond our control'. This invites concentration in a positive way on the ones that can and should be removed in order to make progress towards the agreed objective.

5. Some final points

In order to carry out successful collaborative inquiry it is worth remembering that the following conditions are important:

- a genuinely collaborative atmosphere
- trusting conditions
- an acceptance of the worth of everybody's contribution
- an agreed agenda for discussion and development and/or change
- individual needs and contributions considered as part of the whole
- a sense of being accountable to one another
- a commitment to work together as adult learners in order to enhance the learning environment for all the children in the school.

Part 2

STAFF DEVELOPMENT
MATERIALS

(Help in the Classroom)

Review of Practice

In which areas of our team's/department's/school's practice should we make improvements?

Based on these six statements of principle please ring the rating scale on the basis of:

$\boxed{1}$ needs little or no improvement ⟶ $\boxed{5}$ needs a great deal of improvement.

Classroom assistants should:

i) be clear about their roles and responsibilities	1 2 3 4 5
ii) understand the communication system in the school	1 2 3 4 5
iii) be seen positively as part of the range of provision to meet children's needs	1 2 3 4 5
iv) be members of a working team	1 2 3 4 5
v) be encouraged to make use of their personal skills	1 2 3 4 5
vi) be helped to develop their personal and professional skills alongside other members of staff	1 2 3 4 5

Please hand in to _____

By _____

Thank you.

Help in the Classroom

Action planning questions

As a group or individually you will find it helpful to answer the following questions in the order suggested.

WHAT
- do you intend to do now? (short term objective)
  - as individuals
  - as teachers
  - as assistants
  - as a team?

WHY
- do you intend to do it?
  (Do NOT miss out answering this question - it is of *vital* importance!)

HOW
- do you intend to do it?
  e.g. contact/discussion/meetings/in-service sessions

WHOM
- do you intend to involve in it?
  i.e. just yourselves or others not here now
  e.g.senior management/head/governors/parents/pupils/ INSET Co-ordinator/LEA staff

BY WHEN
- do you intend to have achieved your shorter term objective? How will you know you have?

- do you intend to have achieved your longer term objective?

WHEN
- WILL YOU REVIEW AND EVALUATE?
  (Who will monitor and review?)
  (Who will evaluate and how?)

REMEMBER TO
- State *why* you propose to take the actions you are planning.
- Keep your timescale realistic.
- Put a review/evaluation procedure into place.
- Give everyone a copy of the finalised version.

Help in the Classroom

Action planning outline

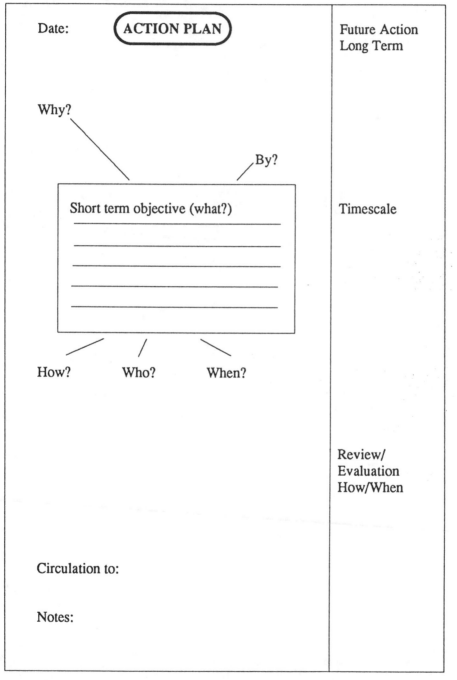

Date: **(ACTION PLAN)**   Future Action
                                     Long Term

Why?

                        By?

Short term objective (what?)   Timescale
_____
_____
_____
_____
_____

How?   Who?   When?

                                     Review/
                                     Evaluation
                                     How/When

Circulation to:

Notes:

Unit 1, Section 1
Co-ordinator's Guidelines

ROLES AND RESPONSIBILITIES

AIM
To develop an understanding of the necessity for a clear job description. This should ensure that assistants and other staff are sure about their responsibilities.

MATERIALS NEEDED
- *Before* session give out pre-session notes to all participants.
- Flipcharts and pens and stand.
- Enough copies of activity sheets for all participants.
- Copies of the action plan outlines and question sheets for all.

GENERAL GUIDELINES

Total Time for Activity: 1 hour

Remind everybody about the aim and their pre-session reading.

Group sizes
- For the discussion activity, groups of 5 or 6.
- Each group, wherever possible, should have an assistant in it (alter group size if necessary).
- Work with flipchart should be done with whole group. Also action planning.

Accommodation
- You need to work in a room that allows for seating to be moved into two or more groups for discussion purposes.
- The whole group should be able to see the flipchart for discussion and action planning.

Level 1 or Level 2 Action Planning?
- Does the action which you are thinking of taking promise to be effective in its own right?
  If so Action Plan at Level 1.
- If you think that something more far reaching is called for with regard to your assistants' roles and responsibilities, plan to move into Section 2 of the materials in this Unit.

Unit1, Section 1
Pre-Session Notes

PIGGY IN THE MIDDLE

Classroom assistants should be clear about their roles and responsibilities.

It is important that schools should recognise the need for assistants to have clearly defined and understood job-descriptions.

When asked about these matters some assistants give examples of spending far too much time unclear about their roles and responsibilities. One described herself as the 'piggy in the middle', caught between the teacher and the children and unclear about how to respond.

There are also examples of assistants who are sure of their role in the school, and are working efficiently as a result. So some schools are definitely able to sort out these areas of potential difficulty for their assistants. Here is an example that you might like to consider:

> 'What we do, we discuss at the end of term and the beginning of the year and get our rota of how we're going to work, and then discuss it with the class teacher - we have meetings every day'.

Assistants who do not receive this level of support are unlikely to work in the most effective ways. If they are confused and uncertain about what they should be doing and why, then they may well feel that much of their time and effort is not being used to the best advantages.

In the activity that follows you will find an opportunity to discuss, with your close colleagues, some of the issues mentioned here, and consider how they relate to the practice in your own school.

Unit 1, Section 1
Activity Materials

ROLES AND RESPONSIBILITIES

Classroom assistants should be clear about their roles and responsibilities.

AIM
To develop an understanding of the necessity for a clear job description. This should ensure that assistants and other staff are sure about their roles and responsibilities.

PIGGY IN THE MIDDLE

Cameo: An assistant describing her lack of guidance.

'Nobody has explained to me properly what I'm supposed to do. I've been picking it up as I go along. Sometimes, but not regularly, I'm given instructions at the start of the day. And I haven't got a proper job description, only a vague one I got with my contract, it's not much practical use. Nobody refers to it anyway, and it's been like this for nearly four terms now'.

Activity:Individually consider the following questions. • What do you think has happened here? • What do you think are the possible causes of the situation described?	**Co-ordinator** Encourage people to think for them selves, rather than comparing notes. (5 minutes)
As a group: • Share your ideas. • Make sure everyone has a turn.	(10 minutes)
Individually or in pairs, consider: • How does this compare with or differ from your own experience individually, or that of your team?	(5 minutes)

As a group:
• *Discuss* briefly these personal experiences in your school.
• Think about the following questions:
   - Why did it happen here?
   - How did I feel about it?
   - What did I/those involved do about it?
   - How might I/those involved have dealt with it differently?
	Co-ordinator
	
	(10 minutes)

As a whole group:
• *Share* these ideas:
• List the causes as you see them on a flipchart.
   - Which of these could be avoided in the future?
   - How might I/we go about preventing them?
• Prioritise some ideas for action.
	
	(10 minutes)

• Co-ordinator: refer here to the guidance on writing out an action plan at Level 1 or moving to Level 2.

Now draw up your action plan. When drawing up your action plan think of the issues you have drawn out in your discussions with regard to your assistants' job descriptions.	**Co-ordinator** Give out individ- ual sheets on action planning - outline - questions.
 • Have they got job descriptions? • When were they last consulted/reviewed? • Are the assistants in any way involved in drawing up or reviewing them?	Use a big version on a flipchart sheet to agree a plan as a group. (Action Planning: 20 minutes)

Use your outline sheet to help you as individuals to contribute to the whole group plan

Unit 1, Section 2
Co-ordinator's Guidelines

ROLES AND RESPONSIBILITIES

AIM

To develop an understanding of the necessity to review practice in any classroom or situation where assistants are involved. Reviewing the role and responsibilities in this way helps to clarify what is working well and why this is so.

MATERIALS NEEDED

- N.B. *before* session give out pre-session notes to *all* participants.
- Flipchart and pens and stand.
- Enough copies of the activity sheets for all participants.
- Copies of the action plan outlines and question sheets for all.

GENERAL GUIDELINES

Total time for activity: 1 hour

Remind everybody about the aim and the pre-session reading.

Group sizes:
- For the discussion activity, groups of 5 or 6.
- Each group, wherever possible, should have an assistant in it (alter group size if necessary).
- Work discussing feedback and action planning should be done with the whole group.

Accommodation:
- You need to work in a room that allows for the seating to be moved into two or more groups for discussion purposes.
- The whole group should be able to see the flipchart for action planning.

PIGGY IN THE MIDDLE

Classroom assistants should be clear about their roles and responsibilities.

It makes sense to review the practice around the roles and responsibilities of assistants. Not only must a clear definition of the role be set out to begin with, but a system of checking how well it is working in each situation/classroom is necessary. This is a whole-school issue, in so far as assistants are seen as a whole-school resource, and anyone who is involved in working directly with assistants should be regularly reviewing their practice. An assistant's description of a recent development helps to make these issues 'come alive':

'Last week we had a meeting involving the assistants and the teachers who work with them, it was timetabled, the deputy head helped over cover, and everybody agreed to manage without their assistants for the last part of the afternoon. We reviewed all the links we had made across the school, where it was working well, where it wasn't. We had a good think about why, tried to pinpoint the way difficulties arose. It was ever so useful, and everybody will now have an individual meeting to discuss with the teacher they work most with, to review their job descriptions, and how the daily routine fits into them, and write something down, so we can review it together at the end of term.

I've been feeling so positive since then, it's great to work and plan with the teachers about what we do. I'm a lot happier now!"

In most schools where there are assistants, quite a number of teaching staff have sessions where they have assistants working with them. Consequently it is important to review the working practice around the roles in each case.

The roles cannot be regarded as static. If the aim for the role is to encourage all pupils to become independent learners, then the changing needs of the pupils will call for changes in the role, and a flexibility in its uses.

Schools which neglect the need for reviewing and monitoring assistants' roles will find that assistants may become less effective in the work they are doing, *through no fault of their own,* but because the 'system' is letting them down. They can then become increasingly dispirited, and lose their way, knowing they could be put to better use, even if they are not quite so sure how!

The job will only develop into a productive one, and therefore a well-used resource for the school, if it is viewed flexibly. In this way it can help to meet the needs of the pupils, the teachers, the curriculum *and* the assistants!

Unit 1, Section 2
Activity Materials

ROLES AND RESPONSIBILITIES

Classroom assistants should be clear about their roles and responsibilities.

AIM

To develop an understanding for the necessity to review practice in any classroom or situation where assistants are involved. Reviewing the role and responsibilities in this way helps to clarify what is working well and why this is so.

PIGGY IN THE MIDDLE

Cameo: A teacher, referring to assistants:

'Why should *we* spend time thinking about special needs assistants? - surely that's the job of the co-ordinator for special needs isn't it? - not us!'

	Co-ordinator
Activity:Individually, bearing in mind the comment above	Remind people that *last* week might be a good one -fresh in the memory! (5 minutes)
• Review a typical working week in your school/ classroom.	
• *Think* of the lessons/sessions when you share a classroom with another adult (teacher or assistant).	
As a group: You will need a person to take notes for the group and a spokesperson.	Reminder about notetaker and spokesperson.
• *List* all the types of activity which the second person of the pair (i.e. the one *not* 'in charge' of the session) has been involved.	
• *Think* of the steps taken beforehand in preparation for these joint activities and list them.	
• How well did both sets of things fit into the assistant's job description? Mark items which have direct relevance for planning and reviewing the role of the assistant.	
• How clear in each set of activities was the role of the assistant to either or both of the pair?	(15 minutes)

As a whole group:
    Listen to the others' feedback.
  • Now you have reviewed your working practice, are there times in the future when you would see a need to review it again?
        - in pairs (classroom sharers)
        - in team groups
        - as a whole staff
  • What actions will people now take as a result?
	Co-ordinator
	(20 minutes)

	Give out individ-
	ual sheets on
	action planning
	    - outline
	    - questions.

Now draw up your Action Plan.
 	
  • Refer to the above questions and the issues you have identified in order to do this.
 	
  • Use your outline sheet to help you as individuals to contribute to the whole.
	Use a big version
	and a flipchart
	sheet to agree a
	plan as a group.
	
	(Action Planning:
	20 minutes)

Unit 2, Section 1
Co-ordinator's Guidelines

COMMUNICATION

AIM
To consider how assistants can be involved in the communication system of the school, and to develop an understanding of the necessity for this.

MATERIALS NEEDED
- N.B. *before* session give out pre-session notes to *all* participants.
- Flipchart and pens and stand.
- Enough copies of the activity sheets for all participants.
- Copies of the action plan outlines and basic questions for all participants.

GENERAL GUIDELINES

(Total time for activity: 1 hour)

Remind everybody about the aim and their pre-session reading.

Group sizes:
- For the brainstorm activity groups of up to 8.
- Work on the action planning should be done with the whole group.

Accommodation:
- A room with the chairs arranged in a circle is best for this activity, where everyone can see the flipchart.

Level 1 or Level 2 Action Planning?
- Does the action which you are thinking of taking promise to be effective in its own right? If so, plan at Level 1.
- If you think that something more fundamental is called for with regard to the assistants' place in the communication system of the school, plan to move into section 2 of the materials in this Unit.

Unit 2, Section 1 Pre-session notes

NO-MAN'S-LAND

Classroom assistants should understand the communication system of the school.

It is important to make sure that assistants are drawn into the communication system of the school. This is of particular importance when assistants work part-time.

Assistants need to know what is happening, or they may find themselves in what one described as 'no-man's-land'. Basic information such as who is visiting the school this week, who is leaving at the end of term, or changes in duty rotas can easily be 'lost' to assistants unless positive steps are taken to draw them into the information system in the school.

Attendance at staff meetings during their contracted hours is one way in which this can be ensured. Attendance at section/departmental meetings held for organisation and planning purposes is also advisable. Making sure that all staff who will be receiving assistant support know about this and are able to plan for it seems a basic point, but it is surprising how often it doesn't happen! Here is an example:

> 'Even now, I go into a class and I have no idea what the lesson is going to be about. How can I get anything ready if I've had no response from the teacher?"

This pinpoints the necessity for reliable systems of communication, of which the assistant is part.

In the activity in which you will be involved you will find the opportunity to look at a small 'cameo' which shows what happened in school after an incident of poor communication. There will be a chance to relate this to experiences and practices in your school.

Unit 2, Section 1 Activity Materials

COMMUNICATION

Classroom assistants should understand the communication system of the school.

AIM
To consider how well the assistants can be involved in the communication system of the school, and to develop an understanding of the necessity for this.

NO-MAN'S-LAND

Cameo: An assistant, describing a breakdown in communication:

'I only found out that Mrs. P was leaving next Friday yesterday. It was really embarrassing because I know *now* that she has to go because the LMS budget isn't enough to pay for everything. I really put my foot in it yesterday. I asked her about who she would be working with next term - it might have been me. She was feeling pretty down about it - and *I* didn't help!

The one good thing about it is, the deputy head's agreed that there should be a list of the main points from the business staff meeting, so that those of us who only work half days, or are ill or something, won't miss out on that kind of news again."

Activity: Individually think about this assistant's description of what happened to her.

	Co-ordinator
• Consider other ways in which she might have been embarrassed or put in a difficult situation by missing out on information - draw on your own experience here.	(5 minutes)
As a group:	
• Brainstorm any ways in which you think a similar situation could arise in your school.	Make sure *everyone* gets a turn here.
• List these on a flipchart.	
• List any 'gaps' you perceive in the communication system of the school as they pertain to you.	
• Assistants be *very* honest here!	(15 minutes) Encourage candid comments.

	Co-ordinator
• Explore possible strategies to avoid them (the gaps).	
• List these on a flipchart.	(15 minutes)
• Prioritise them in a way which suits you as a group.	
Here are two suggestions, you may prefer something different:	(10 minutes)
either: those which would be easy to avoid by taking minimal action for immediate results,	
or: those which you feel would avoid the 'worst' potential incidences, particularly for assistants, by taking action.	

• Co-ordinator: refer here to the guidance on working out an action plan at Level 1 or moving to Level 2.

Now draw up your action plan.	**Co-ordinator**

When drawing up your action plan think of the priorities you have identified during your discussions.	Give out individual sheets on action planning
	    - outline
	    - questions.

• Can you plug any identified 'gaps' and if so, how?	Use a big version on a flipchart sheet to agree a plan as a group.
• How can any other improvements be made?	
• What are the 'good' areas of the communication system - can we extend them?	(Action Planing: 15 minutes)

Unit 2, Section 2
Co-ordinator's Guidelines

COMMUNICATION

AIM
To examine the school's communication system with particular respect to the role in it of classroom assistants.

MATERIALS NEEDED
- N.B. *Before* session give out pre-session notes to *all* participants.
- Flipchart and pens and stands.
- Enough copies of the activity sheets for all participants.
- Copies of the action plan outlines and basic questions for all participants.
- Your instructions for managing Nominal Group Technique.

GENERAL GUIDELINES

Total time for activity: 1 hour 30 minutes

Remind everybody about the aim and their pre-session reading.

Group sizes:
- For the discussion and Nominal Group Technique up to 8 people, including at least one assistant.
- If you need more than one group you should prepare a colleague *beforehand* to lead Nominal Group Technique.

Accommodation:
- Enough room to arrange the chairs into more than one group as necessary.
- The whole group should be able to see the flipchart for action planning.

Unit 2, Section 2
Pre-session notes

NO-MAN'S-LAND

Classroom assistants should understand the communication system of the school.

It may be necessary to review the school practice with regards to communication with *and* about the assistants working there. Not only do assistants need to be aware of what is going on (at all kinds of levels), but other people need to know about them - why they are there, what they do, and how they fit in. An assistant's description of an incident that happened to her illustrates the need for this to be considered, and the crucial question of 'who' should know 'what' comes to the fore.

> 'The other thing is, when you have lessons and they've got cover, like I had on Friday last week. We had French, the member of staff had *no* idea about French, the children had got work to do, so you know, who goes round to help them? I do! and you know, I don't mind, but I think "*Well* the teaching staff are getting *five times* the amount of money I'm getting!"'

Amongst people who need to know about assistants, who they are, and what they do, are the school staff who do not regularly or presently have assistant support in the normal timetable, and supply teachers, internal and external. Parents, who should also know, may ask why they are there, as should governors and other professionals such as speech therapists and physiotherapists. You will probably be able to think of others to whom this would apply who either work in or visit your school.

   The following activity will help you to think about the communication system in the school and where your assistants fit into this.

Help in the classroom

Unit 2, Section 2 Activity Materials

COMMUNICATION

Classroom assistants should understand the communication system of the school.

AIM

To examine the school's communication system with particular respect to the role of the classroom assistant.

NO-MAN'S-LAND

Cameo: An assistant, describing an unfortunate incident:

'Sometimes we are in a really difficult position. It's about "officialdom" - where does it end? How much should I say or should the teacher say? A parent was in the other day - she more or less pinned me up against the wall, and insisted on me giving her some information. I didn't know enough about it, but wasn't sure to tell her or not anyway. She didn't seem to realise that it was perhaps the head's job to do this - she also said "Well, who are you, if you can't tell me?" So I explained... it was *really* embarrassing!'

	Co-ordinator
Activity: As a group: • Tease out the issues that underlie this somewhat complex and embarrassing situation. • Who should have known about what? • Why do you think they didn't?	(10 minutes)
Individually: • Think of experiences/situations in your school which have any similarities to the one above.	(5 minutes)
As a group: Using Nominal Group Technique consider the following questions: • How can the school's communication system be improved?	Refer here to the guidelines on managing Nominal Group Technique. (45 minutes)

You will then be able to identify priorities for action.

Now draw up your Action Plan.
Using the priorities identified from your master list, and keeping in mind both aspects
  • What assistants should know
  • What others should know about them
 	
Now plan your way ahead.
	Co-ordinator
	Give out individual sheets on action planning
	    - outline
	    - questions.
	Use a big version on the flipchart to plan as a group.
	(Action Planning: 30 minutes)

Unit 3, Section 1
Co-ordinator's Guidelines

CONSISTENCY OF APPROACH

AIM
To examine how two adults sharing a classroom in order to meet the needs of the children can work most effectively.

MATERIALS NEEDED
- N.B. *Before* session give out pre-session notes to *all* participants.
- Flipchart and pens and stand.
- Enough copies of the activity sheets for all participants.
- Copies of the action plan outlines and question sheet for all participants.

GENERAL GUIDELINES

(**Total time for activity: 1 hour**)

Remind everyone about the aim and their pre-session reading.

Group sizes:
- For the activity, groups of 5 or 6 including at least one assistant.
- For Action Planning, the whole group.

Accommodation:
- You need to work in a room that allows for smaller groups to be formed if necessary.
- The whole group should be able to see the large action planning sheet.

Level 1 or Level 2 Action Planning?
- Does the action you are thinking of taking promise to be effective in its own right? If so, action plan at Level 1.
- If you think something more radical is called for with regard to the way in which the school manages working partnerships and consistency of approaches in classrooms, plan to move into Section 2 of the materials in this Unit.

Unit 3, Section 1
Pre-session notes

DOGSBODY

Classroom assistants should be seen positively as part of the range of provision to meet children's needs.

It is important that assistants should be employed in a consistent and productive manner in the school. They should not experience the feeling of being a 'general dogsbody' - which is the way at least one assistant has described herself.

It is particularly difficult if assistants find enormous differences in the way they are expected to work between teachers. Of course, working practice *is* almost bound to vary to some degree, because of differing personalities and teaching styles. However, there should be an agreed set of 'groundrules'. This takes you back to the importance of job description and its 'interpretation' by various teachers. A teacher explains some of the issues:

> 'We're clear about who's doing what before we start, because we've worked out a pattern for different situations, depending on what I'm teaching. I've also talked to Mrs P about it, so when the assistant goes into her lessons on Tuesdays and Fridays she finds a similar pattern of working, but does quite different things with the children. With me she does work on topics and cross-curricular themes. Mrs P has her working on more basic curriculum areas, language and maths for example.'

A flexibility in what is done in certain aspects is obvious here, but the main 'groundrules' appear to be clear to all. This must mean that the assistant is able to be more effective, as she is being asked to work in a consistent way.

In the activity session there is an opportunity to examine some of the issues that arise when adults share classrooms. Of particular importance here are aspects that need to be considered before sharing a classroom. Such collaborations are unlikely to be successful by good luck, and it will not do to assume 'it will be alright on the night' - it is not the West End!

Unit 3, Section 1
Activity Materials

CONSISTENCY OF APPROACH

Classroom assistants should be seen positively as part of the range of provision to meet children's needs.

AIM

To examine how two adults, sharing a classroom in order to meet the needs of the children, can work most effectively.

(DOGSBODY)

Cameo: An assistant describing her anxieties about something planned for the next half term:

'I'm going to support in Mrs M's class after half term because some of the children have moved on. She's never worked with anybody in the classroom before. She stuck out to be left out of the team teaching that was set up last year. It's a shame these children I need to work with are in *her* class, but they *do* need some support. I *hope* it'll be alright!'

'Sharing Classroom' activity:	**Co-ordinator**
• *Individually* consider the situation described by the assistant	Encourage people to think individually here before chatting.

• *Think* of all the potential difficulties arising for
      - Mrs M
      - the assistant
      - the children.
	(5 minutes)

As a group:	
• *Share* your ideas about the problems you foresee for Mrs M, the assistant, the children.	
• *List* them on the flipchart.	(15 minutes)

D

	Co-ordinator

• Then attempt to *identify* the problems which could be generalised to other situations when two adults are sharing a classroom.
• *Mark* them * on the list.
• *Think* of the things you are planning to do in the school in the next few weeks/next term that you feel might be made more successful by having considered the issues you have marked.
• *Attempt* to draw up a set of groundrules that you would find useful for:
   - the teacher(s)
   - the assistant(s)
   - the children.
	(20 minutes)

Share these groundrules if you have been working in more than one group.

• Co-ordinator: refer here to the guidance on working out an action plan at Level 1 or moving to Level 2.

Now draw up your Action Plan.
When doing this, think about how to implement your 'groundrules'.

	Co-ordinator
• Which are the most important? • Which could you do reasonably easily and swiftly? • Are there some you could try out in working pairs?	Give out individual sheets on action planning - outline - questions. Use a big version and a flipchart sheet to agree a plan as a group. (Action Planning: 20 minutes)

Use your outline sheet as individuals to contribute to the whole group plan

Help in the classroom

Unit 3, Section 2
Co-ordinator's Guidelines

CONSISTENCY OF APPROACH

AIM
To encourage staff to see classroom assistants as a positive resource that should be used consistently to meet children's needs.

MATERIALS NEEDED
- N.B. *Before* session give out pre-session notes to *all* participants.
- Flipchart and green, red and black pens and stand.
- Enough copies of the activity sheets for all participants.
- Copies of the action plan outlines and question sheet for all participants.
- 'Brick Wall' outlines - enough for everyone.
- A flipchart (large) version of the 'Brick Wall' outline.

GENERAL GUIDELINES

(Total time for activity: 1 hour 20 minutes)

Remind everyone about the aims and their pre-session reading.

Group size:
- For the 'Brick Wall' activity the whole group if possible. If it is too big then split into two groups and do a pairing of the two groups' 'Brick Wall'.
- For action planning, the whole group.

Accommodation:
- You need to work in a room where more than one group can be arranged from the seating.
- The whole group should be able to see the 'Brick Wall' sheet and Action Planning sheet on the flipchart.

Unit 3, Section 2
Pre-session Notes

DOGSBODY

Classroom assistants should be seen positively as part of the range of provision to meet children's needs.

It is well worth considering drawing up a set of 'groundrules' to help to create consistency throughout the school. However these will probably only go part of the way towards reducing inconsistency.

Underlying deep-rooted inconsistencies in using assistants as a resource, are uncertainties felt by individuals about what the job is about, at a much more fundamental level. A whole school policy worked out by the school is the key to reducing these uncertainties.

Attitudes and perceptions can make or break school policy. The vision and purpose in the school about its approaches to special educational needs should be clear and agreed by all the people working in and for the school. Underlying attitudes about special educational needs can create a great deal of inconsistency in both policy and practice, and this will inevitably have an impact on the working lives of the assistants. If assistants are seen as a positive part of the range of provision to meet children's needs, they will be less likely to experience the situation described here:

> "The English teacher I've worked with has been very helpful, she has been very nice as a person, because some of the staff won't accept me for what we are - if they could be 100 per cent honest, don't want us in the classroom."

It is important to recognise that such differing attitudes and stances about provision to meet children's needs, including assistants, often do exist in schools. These should be acknowledged and accounted for in considering how the assistants should work. If assistants are viewed positively as part of the provision then they are unlikely to experience great inconsistencies in approach to them and their work.

The activity that follows should help all participants to consider these important issues, particularly in relation to assistants, and their place in the policy of the school.

Unit 3, Section 2 Activity Material

CONSISTENCY OF APPROACH

Classroom assistants should be seen positively as part of the range of provision to meet children's needs.

AIM
To encourage staff to see classroom assistants as a positive resource that should be used consistently to meet children's needs.

DOGSBODY

Cameo: A teacher:

'It doesn't matter if they have their break in the secretary's office, the staffroom's too small as it is, for all the teachers.'

An assistant:

'The atmosphere in the staffroom can be difficult, it depends on which teachers are there. Some would probably prefer us not to be there, others welcome us as "one of the staff"'.

'Brick Walls' Activity	Co-ordinator
• Individually consider what is getting in the way of consistency of approaches in the above situation. • Has it, or something similar, happened in your school?	Encourage people to think about this alone before chatting.
• Using the 'Brick wall' outline think of all the things in your school that get in the way of achieving the objective behind the wall. • Fill these in (simply - a word or a phrase) on the blank bricks on your wall. These represent 'blocks' - what gets in the way. Do it *without* discussing it.	(5 minutes) Give out the 'Brick Wall'outlines.
• It is not necessary to fill in *every* block!!	(15 minutes) People may like to chat in pairs before whole group task.

	Co-ordinator
As a group: • On the large duplicate Brick Wall blank build up a *group Brick Wall* by taking a 'block' from each member of the group in turn. If more than one person has the same 'block' put a mark in the brick (each time it is duplicated).	Brick Wall on flipchart needed here. (20 minutes)

Discuss the 'blocks' using the following questions to guide you:
• Are there any 'blocks' that we can remove immediately by taking some action?
  - as individuals (teachers/assistants)
  - together as a team?
Mark these with a green tick.
• Are there any 'blocks' we feel we can do nothing about - they are 'beyond our control'- at least for the present? (So let's not worry about what we can do nothing about!)
Mark these with a red cross
• Are there any 'blocks' we feel we could work at removing over a period of time?
  - as individuals (teachers/assistants)
  - together as a team.
Mark these with a green question mark.
	(20 minutes)

Now draw up your Action Plan. You have already identified priorities for the short term action(s) and longer term ones.	Give out individual sheets on action planning. - outline - questions
When drawing up the group action plan, build thesein.	Use big version of action plan on flipchart. 20 minutes)
Individuals may like to return to their individual walls and check to see if there is some personal action they can take, as well as what is agreed on the group action plan.	Keep the group 'Brick Wall' - you may well wish to refer to it again when reviewing progress with your action plan.

Objective: Classroom assistants should be seen positively as part of a range of provision to meet children's needs.

Unit 4, Section 1
Co-ordinator's Guidelines

A WORKING TEAM

AIM
To consider how assistants may be involved as members of a working team, through information sharing and problem solving. In this context every member's contribution is valued as having inherent worth.

MATERIALS NEEDED
- *Before* session give out pre-session notes to *all* participants.
- Flipchart and pens and stand.
- Enough copies of the activity sheets for all participants.
- Copies of the action plan outlines and question sheet for all participants.
- A set of strips (or 2 sets) about 'Tom' to be distributed round the group(s) (photocopied onto card and cut up prior to session).

GENERAL GUIDELINES

Total time for activity: 1 hour 20 minutes

Remind everyone about the aim and their pre-session reading.

Group sizes:
- For the activity, groups of about 6 or 7 are best, including at least one assistant in each group.
- For action planning, the whole group.

Accommodation:
- You need to arrange the chairs in a way that helps verbal communication in small groups.
- The whole group should be able to see the large action planning sheet.

Level 1 or Level 2 Action Planning?
- Does the action which you are thinking of taking promise to be effective in its own right? If so, Action Plan at Level 1.
- If you think something more fundamental is called for with regard to the way the whole school team, including the assistants, shares information and solves problems, plan to move into Section 2 of the materials in this Unit.

SPY IN THE CLASSROOM

Classroom assistants should be part of a working team.

The focus of this section is the assistants' place in both the whole school team and the immediate working team.

The experience of being kept at a distance, 'on the margins', is not conducive to a positive working atmosphere and good working relationships. It has even occasioned the response 'I feel like a spy in the classroom' - it seems impossible to imagine informed, constructive classroom observation using the adults in a positive collaborative way given the situation.

An involvement in planning the programme for joint working - teacher/assistant and assistant/pupil, is essential if effort and resources are to pay off. This planning should be seen as an investment, done in working time, and not as a 'bolt-on' nuisance, even a luxury. It should be carried out in such a way as to value everybody's contribution. When this is the norm in a school then the following comment is likely:

> 'We work as a team very much, and I am allowed a lot of freedom, which I must say I do like. I like to be able to feel I'm actually thinking for myself, albeit I can always talk it over with the teachers.'

This assistant obviously feels she is very much part of the team. It seems very positive, indicating trust in the assistant to use her skills, but offering support when she needs it.

In the activity in which you will be involved you will find an opportunity to consider the necessity for assistants to be part of the team, involved in sharing information and planning, as equal members.

Unit 4, Section 1
Activity Materials

A WORKING TEAM

Classroom assistants should be part of a working team.

AIM
To consider how assistants may be involved as members of a working team, through information sharing and problem solving. In this context every member's contribution is valued as having inherent worth.

A SPY IN THE CLASSROOM

Cameo: An assistant's observation:

'I think if some teachers were 100% honest they would admit that they think of us all as "second class citizens", and they just can't see the potential we have to offer as part of the team.'

Activity - "Tom"
   Bearing in mind the above comment, and with the idea of information sharing and problem solving in mind you will now be considering the story of "Tom". This activity will help you to think about the team's information sharing and problem solving strategies.

As a group:
- Share the cards out evenly amongst the group, randomly, face down.
- Do not allow anyone to see what is written on the cards you are dealt.
- Share the information on the cards verbally. Do not:
   - show them to each other,
   - put them in the middle of the group or
   - write down on a corporate list.
- You may make notes for your own personal use.

Co-ordinator
Make sure the instructions are clearly understood - clarify any issues or questions.

	Co-ordinator
On the cards you each have a range of information, some of which is useful, some of which are red herrings.	
As a group you need to pool the information and come to some decisions about course(s) of action which might be taken given the situation presented to you. The question is:'What should the school and the individuals be doing about Tom?'.	(30 minutes)
After 30 minutes, and having made some decisions about possible courses of action, debrief the activity (either in the small groups or in the larger group).	
Debrief Briefly describe the course of action your group decided on and why that was so.	Keep this brief. (5 minutes)
Spend *more* time on considering what you learnt from the process you went through - information sharing and problem solving - what have you individually learnt? - what as a group did you learn?	The *process* issues are important here. (15 minutes)

As a group:
- Now consider your course of action with regards to sharing information and developing team problem solving. Base your decision making for action on the issues you have been considering and how every member of the team could be part of the plan of action for you as a team.

• Co-ordinator: refer here to the guidance on working out an action plan at Level 1 or moving to Level 2.

Now draw up your Action Plan.
Consider the following points:
- It will help to identify a current problem in the school which requires the approach of a corporate effort in order to tackle it. It may help to put this on a flipchart.

- State why you think this problem needs tackling.
  Think carefully about your timescale.
- Consider how you will review progress with your Action Planning and problem solving.

Co-ordinator
Give out individual sheets on action planning
 - outline
 - questions.
Use a big version on a flipchart sheet to agree a plan as a group.

(Action Planning: 30 minutes)

'TOM'

Miss Sterne is very insistent on children arriving in time for school.

Tom has difficulty getting up in the morning.

Tom's older sister experienced a lot of problems in school.

Tom Atkinson is nine.

On the Salford Reading Test Tom has a reading age of 6.5

Tom's artwork is outstanding.

At home Tom spends a lot of time playing computer games.

Mrs. Jones reports that Tom has been very difficult in her groups.

Mrs. Atkinson gets very lonely during the day.

Tom's best friend George is in the infant department.

Tom goes to Cubs on Tuesday evenings.

Tom dislikes lessons where the teacher does a lot of talking to the class.

Tom gets sent to Miss Sterne for misbehaving sometimes.

Tom misses out on rewards like the computer or robot games.

Tom's concentration on written tasks is very poor.

Jenny says Tom hit her twice yesterday.

Tom has great difficulty in following class instructions.

The extra reading help that he has received for the last three years does not seem to have worked with Tom.

Tom's Grandad has just bought him a Subbuteo game.

Mrs Jenkins, the assistant, enjoys doing art with the children.

Tom loves his dog.

Recently Tom's dog has been ill.

Mrs. Jones takes Tom for reading three times a week.

Tom's father died when he was two years old.

Mrs. Atkinson sometimes works on a night shift in a factory.

Tom is a keen Liverpool fan.

Mr. Roberts, Tom's teacher, insists on silence in the class when pupils are doing maths.

Tom is very overweight.

Tom's teacher believes in rigorous P.E. lessons.

Tom is not popular with most of the other children in the class.

Unit 4, Section 2
Co-ordinator's Guidelines

A WORKING TEAM

AIM
To examine the staff's development with regard to including the assistants in an effective working team, at whole school level.

MATERIALS NEEDED
- *Before* session give out pre-session notes to *all* participants.
- Flipchart and pens and stand.
- Enough copies of the activity sheets for all participants.
- Copies of the action plan outlines and question sheet for all participants.
- Enough copies of the 'Memo Exercise' sheet for all and box(es) to put sheets in.

GENERAL INSTRUCTIONS

(Total time for activity: 1 hour)

Remind everyone about the aim and their pre-session reading.

Group sizes:
- Up to 8 in a group for the Memo Exercise with at least one assistant in each group.
- For action planning, the whole group.

Accommodation:
- You need to work in a room that allows for the seating to be arranged in smaller groups if the maximum number is more than 8.
- The whole group should be able to see the large action planning sheet.

Help in the classroom

Unit 4, Section 2
Pre-session Notes

SPY IN THE CLASSROOM

Classroom assistants should be members of a working team.

There may well be a need to review the school's practice with regard to how it involves assistant(s) in the whole-school team.

Overall membership of the wider school team is a positive step much as creating a feeling of 'belonging' to a particular working group (often a partnership). Involvement in information sharing, decision making and planning is a way of fostering this team membership at a whole school level, particularly if it takes place inside assistants contracted hours.

Attitudinal stances with regard to the value of the assistant's contributions may well get in the way of this. These include professionalism ('they're not qualified and we are'), and perceptions of status and hierarchy, which can pose a very real difficulty in team development.

Part of being in effective teams, and indeed the way they develop, is by being listened to and having one's opinion valued. 'Spies in the classroom' as an assistant was heard to say, do not tend to feel valued for their contribution to the whole! Much more positive is the following description, offered by an assistant about being in an effective team:

> 'We've been working at objectives or targets for each of us for the lessons, and learning how is the best way to review that. At staff meetings the successes and failures have been talked about and we've drawn up some helpful guidelines for anybody to use. It's really good, and one of *my* ideas is in there!'

An assistant feeling positive about the contribution to a team development made by herself is likely to feel very much part of a developing team.

In the following activity there is an opportunity to help people to be honest about what they think of how the team *could* develop, and for you to make your contributions to this discussion.

Unit 4, Section 2
Activity Materials

A WORKING TEAM

Classroom assistants should be members of a working team.

AIM
To examine the staff's development with regard to including the assistants in an effective working team, at whole-school level.

A SPY IN THE CLASSROOM

Cameo: An assistant:

'I'm not sure that if we each tried to explain what we're trying to do as a team the explanations and reasons would be the same. People assume... but you find it's not always as open as you think.'

'Memo Exercise' Activity
To allow some consideration of the above issues in a non-threatening way 'anonymous' memos will be written and then examined by everybody as a group. Clarification and discussion should result in some clarity and openness about the issues raised.

Individually: • Group members fill in the 'Memo Exercise' sheet they have been given. • These should then be placed in a box. *As a group:* • Each person in the group should then pick out a 'Memo' sheet, read it to the group and make a comment in response to 'set the ball rolling'. If people pick out their own, they should put them back and take another.	**Co-ordinator** (15 minutes)

Help in the classroom

	Co-ordinator
• Discuss each of the 'Memos' in turn.	
• Consider the implications of each of the statements - are they raising previously unknown difficulties or issues for people?	(25 minutes)
Is there anything that suggests immediate action that:	Give out individual sheets on action planning
• one person could take?	- outline
• a group of people could take?	- questions.
• the whole school might work on?	Use a big version and a flipchart sheet to agree a plan as a group.
	(Action Planning: 20 minutes)
Now draw up an Action Plan.	

MEMO EXERCISE

Complete the following sentence with three (maximum) suggestions.

In order for our team to work well, I would like...

-

-

-

Think of the things *you* would like to do to contribute.

Think of the things you think other people either ought to do, or perhaps could think about.

Think about the team as a whole - what would you like it to do?

Unit 5, Section 1
Co-ordinator's Guidelines

USING PERSONAL SKILLS

AIM
To consider how best the skills of everybody in the working team can be used with regard to a particular area of the curriculum. To 'unpack' the skills, talents, likes and dislikes of the team members.

MATERIALS NEEDED
- *Before* session give out pre-session notes to *all* participants.
- Flipchart and pens and stand.
- Enough copies of the activity sheets for all participants.
- Copies of the action plan outlines and question sheet for all participants.

GENERAL INSTRUCTIONS

(Total time for activity: 1 hour 15 minutes)

Remind everyone about the aim and their pre-session reading.

Group sizes:
- The whole group after discussing in 2's/3's.
- The whole group for action planning.

Accommodation:
- The seating should be adaptable so chairs can be moved into small groups for 2 or 3 people to work together.
- The whole group should be able to see the guidelines/questions sheet and Action Plan on the flipchart.

Level 1 or Level 2 Action Planning?
- Does the action which you are thinking of taking promise to be effective in its own right?
  If so, Action Plan at Level 1.
- If you think something more fundamental is called for with regard to using everybody's skills more effectively in the whole school team in order to diversify curriculum approaches, plan to move into Section 2 of the materials in this Unit.

Unit 5, Section 1
Pre-Session Notes

OVERGROWN PUPIL

Classroom assistants should be encouraged to make use of their personal skills.

It is advisable that schools attempt to make sure that people's strengths and skills are used positively, in a way that enhances the learning environment.

Wasted talent amongst the adults working in the school is unfortunate and limits the overall range of responses available to meet children's needs. An assistant who feels like an 'overgrown pupil' is hardly in a helpful situation, and this is unlikely to lead to a productive use of talents. An exploration of what everybody is able to offer to a situation (within the team development and planning meetings) is likely to pay off in extending broad and balanced curriculum approaches to pupils.

A supportive relationship, fostered in the team development meetings also allows for 'weaknesses' or worries to be acknowledged, accounted for and supported.

An assistant offers here what one sees as an important contribution she would have been able to make, if somebody had asked her!

> "I feel that because I've got children of my own, who've just been through *that* stage, I could help with suggesting ideas. The school they're at did some really interesting things which Lucy responded to very positively. I could see those two we've been having difficulty with recently would have been enthusiastic about a different approach, you know, they'd be much less bored."

A discussion where different ideas were asked for and considered, would no doubt have helped a sensible suggestion to be brought forward, and possibly used within a range of approaches, in this situation.

In the activity that follows there is the opportunity to explore the ideas and skills of everybody in the immediate team, with the intention of enhancing the learning environment, for all of its pupils.

Unit 5, Section 1
Activity Materials

USING PERSONAL SKILLS

> **Classroom assistants should be encouraged to make use of their personal skills.**
>
> ### AIM
> To consider how best the skills of everybody in the working team can be used with regard to a particular area of the curriculum. To 'unpack' the skills, talents, likes and dislikes of the team members.
>
> ## OVERGROWN PUPIL
>
> *Cameo:*Some comments that assistants have made:
>
> 'All this observation that has to be done for the National Curriculum, I could help with a lot more of that...'
>
> 'I worked on the National Trust's group that helped to restore that section of canal...'
>
> 'I know it's a long time since I got my swimming certificate, but...'
>
> 'I did 'O' level French at night class in 1985...'
>
> ### Curriculum review activity
>
> | In two's and three's: | Co-ordinator |
> |---|---|
> | • Consider a recent piece of work carried out by teacher(s) and assistant(s) in the classroom, on a curriculum area (e.g. a series of maths lessons, some cross-curricular topic work, or a 'one-off' activity) bearing in mind some of the above comments. | (5 minutes maximum to decide) |

E

	Co-ordinator
Some questions to help your thinking: • How well did it work? • How were each of the adults utilised? • Were all the skills you could each have used put to good effect?	(20 minutes to analyse)
Make some statements: • With hindsight I... • With hindsight we...	(10 minutes to write statements)
As a group: • Generate a set of questions or guidelines you could run through to guide yourselves, using the benefit of hindsight, in your next piece(s) of curriculum planning. • Put these onto the flipchart.	(20 minutes)

• Co-ordinator: refer here to the guidance on working out an action plan at Level 1 or moving to Level 2.

	Co-ordinator
Now draw up your Action Plan. Draw up an action plan to put these questions/guidelines into effect within your working team(s) Decide which particular piece of the curriculum you will plan for and make that the short term objective so you have a clear focus.	Give out individual sheets on action planning - outline - questions. Use a big version and a flipchart sheet to agree a plan as a group. (Action Planning: 20 minutes)

Unit 5, Section 2
Co-ordinator's Guidelines

USING PERSONAL SKILLS

AIM
To create an atmosphere in which people are able to explore their contributions to the learning environment of the school, in ways that will facilitate the progress of all pupils.

MATERIALS NEEDED
- *Before* session give out pre-session notes to *all* participants.
- Flipchart and pens and stand.
- Enough copies of the activity sheets for all participants.
- Copies of the action plan outlines and question sheet for all participants.
- Copies of the 'Observers Schedule' (according to number of groups)

GENERAL INSTRUCTIONS

> **Total time for activity: 1 hour (minimum)**

Remind everyone about the aim and their pre-session reading.

Group sizes:
- 5 in a group is about the best ratio for the Visitor exercise. Pairs plus observer is the minimum.
  Debrief in same groups.

Accommodation:
- You will need one or more separate rooms with furniture which can be arranged by the group themselves.
- A room arranged so everyone can see the large sheet for the Action Planning.

Unit 5, Section 2
Pre-Session Notes

OVERGROWN PUPIL

Classroom assistants should be encouraged to make use of their personal skills.

The issue of capitalising on the talents of all members of the school, including assistants, to enhance the learning environment for its pupils, begs the question - how do we establish what talents are available in a way which is sensitive and realistic? Assistants who feel like 'an overgrown pupil' obviously have not had the chance to explore these issues, and are unlikely to feel that they are able to offer much to the overall resources the school has to offer its pupils.

However, an assistant who is encouraged, with others in the team, to explore the way in which the talents and skills they have can be used *and* developed is likely to become confident in order to try new ideas to build on.

> 'I have quite a lot of ideas about how to work in the next bit of the National Curriculum, especially where I could bring some things we've collected at home... the trouble is, we aren't asked to contribute in that kind of way. I don't want to sit in a corner with one or two children with worksheets, it's so boring. I find it boring, so I'm sure they do!'

This assistant is clearly itching to have a go at doing something more adventurous and less boring. It is unfortunate that the school has not realised what a wasted resource they appear to have.

Exploring resources of the human kind is the focus of the next activity, taking account of skills, opinions, likes and dislikes of all the staff, including assistants.

Unit 5, Section 2 Activity Materials

USING PERSONAL SKILLS

Classroom assistants should be encouraged to make use of their personal skills.

AIM
To create an atmosphere in which people are able to explore their contributions to the learning environment of the school, in ways that will facilitate the progress of all pupils.

Cameo: A teacher about an assistant:

'She's just an assistant, she shouldn't be asked to help with planning the topic work we're going to cover in science and humanities.'

The assistant thinks:

'But I haven't had the chance to tell her about the work I've done with the nature conservancy organisation - that would be very useful for this topic.'

A 'Visitor' exercise
This activity allows each member of the group to have the 'platform'.

Considering the above scenario, and the perceived waste of talent and dismissive nature of the teacher's comment, this activity seeks to help you as a team to examine the skills, talents, likes, dislikes, etc. of your team members, and them to capitalise on them.

Co-ordinator: If you have a group of two, it is helpful to enlist at least one extra person to be involved in this exercise, either within the discussion or as an 'observer' to debrief.

Larger groups may also choose to have an observer and there is an observation schedule attached which you can use to debrief the group processes.

	Co-ordinator
The chosen visitor (or volunteer) leaves the room and the rest of the group prepare to receive the 'visitor' into the group as a guest .	Have the observer schedules ready for anyone needing them.

The group has to decide on how:
- To put the visitor at ease.
- To elicit as much information as possible without appearing to 'grill' the visitor.
- To agree which roles they will each perform and the questions they will put.

The following list helps the discussion:
- Likes and dislikes about the job.
- personal opinions, preferences, etc.
- Hopes and fears about the job.
- Interests outside school.
- Unfulfilled wishes (you might have a once hopeful Olympic Swimmer in your midst!)
- Something never done at work, but would like to try.
- Something which might help improve working life.

This discussion should take *no longer* than ten minutes and less if there is only a pair to discuss with the visitor.	(10 minutes preparation)

Invite the visitor in and conduct your activity as you have planned it.
Debrief:
  • How did the 'visitor' feel?
  • How did the rest of the group feel?
  • What did the observer see?
  • What have you learnt about individuals in the team?
	(20 minutes)
	
	The debriefing should take place each 'visitor' session.
	(10 minutes)

Now draw up your Action Plan	**Co-ordinator**
Bearing in mind curriculum planning at present being undertaken in the school/team/department	Give out individual sheets on action planning
• how do you now feel you can best use the skills and talents of both assistants and teachers in the future?	-outline - questions
Use some of the key areas (objectives) each person has described which might for them as individuals, and for the team, improve	Use a big version and a flipchart sheet to agree a plan as a group.
• practice in the classroom • job satisfaction. • Identify good practice which can be built on.	(Action Planning: 20 minutes)

OBSERVATION SCHEDULE

Decision making period
- How were the decisions reached about how the session should go?

- Who took the lead?

'Visitor' in the group
- How 'comfortable' did the visitor appear to be?
  - initially?

  - throughout the session?

- In what ways did the group members elicit the information they sought?

- How much did they encourage dialogue rather than 'interrogation'?

- How well did they appear to achieve their objectives?

- Further comments (objective) about approaches to the task
  e.g. listening, encouraging etc.

Unit 6, Section 1
Co-ordinator's Guidelines

STAFF DEVELOPMENT NEEDS

AIM

To identify staff development (INSET) needs, both in terms of the way people like to learn, as well as what they want to learn. This includes a recognition that learning 'on the job' can be a very effective method.

MATERIALS NEEDED
- *Before* session give out pre-session notes to *all* participants.
- Flipchart and pens and stand.
- Enough copies of the activity sheets for all participants.
- Copies of the action plan outlines and question sheet for all participants.
- Envelopes containing sets of cards cut from photocopied sheets (enough for each participant) for 'card sorting' activity.

GENERAL INSTRUCTIONS

> **Total time for activity: 1 hour 10 minutes**

Remind everyone about the aim and their pre-session reading.

Group sizes:
- For sorting activity, individuals, then 2's (then 4's each with an assistant in the group).
- Whole group for negotiation and action planning.

Accommodation:
- A table or floor space is needed for individual sorting activity. Pairs and fours need space to compare their results.
- The whole group should be able to see the flipchart for negotiation and action planning.

Level 1 or Level 2 Action Planning?
- Does the action which you are thinking of taking promise to be effective in its own right? If so, Action Plan at Level 1.
- If you think something more fundamental is called for with regard to the staff development programme in the school, and including assistants in it positively, plan to move into Section 2 of the materials in this Unit.

Unit 6, Section 1
Pre-Session Notes

LEFT UP IN THE AIR

Classroom assistants should be helped to develop their personal and professional skills alongside other members of staff.

It is helpful to consider ways of developing the immediate group of staff in which the assistant works in order to create an atmosphere in which all the team are able to learn together.

The team spends much of its time working in classrooms and effective in-service training can and does take place in classrooms, given the right atmosphere, and the recognition of the need for it.

Assistants and teachers can develop new skills and practice together through examining their working day - or part of it! This can be done in a constructively critical way, trying out new ideas and approaches together and learning as a result. They may well benefit from this approach as may the children.

Assistants who are 'left up in the air', feeling they have identified a need for some in-service training are unlikely to work as positively as those who have had a need identified *and* supported, through either school-based work or external courses.

An assistant experiencing the following situation would probably consider herself to have been 'left up in the air'.

> 'It was useful, that last course, but there are things it doesn't help, about how we work in school. It's all very well doing some of the things we did on the course back in school. I've tried some and they've been really useful. What it doesn't do though, is get under the skin of what happens to me in school - in the last week we were talking about somebody who had been to several staff or team meetings because they wanted her to be in on the curriculum things they were doing. I can't imagine that happening here unless things change...'

The following activity encourages the working team to explore how staff development (INSET) needs are identified and can be met. It examines the use of resources from within school, as well as from outside. It also considers how these can be used in ways that are more relevant and practical.

Unit 6, Section 1 Activity Materials

STAFF DEVELOPMENT NEEDS

> **Classroom assistants should be helped to develop their personal and professional skills alongside other members of staff.**
>
> **AIM**
> To identify staff development (INSET) needs, both in terms of the way people like to learn, as well as what they want to learn. This includes a recognition that learning 'on the job' can be a very effective method.
>
> ### LEFT UP IN THE AIR
>
> *Cameo:*   A statement by an assistant:
>
> 'I went to my in-service course on Wednesday afternoons, and I don't normally work on Wednesday afternoons! I gave that up out of my own time to go on the course, and I think that in a way if you've taken time to do this it might be recognised somewhere along the line...'
>
> **'Card Sorting' Activity**
> The aim of this activity is to attempt to avoid the situation above, (or something similar). It does this by examining some forms of staff development and people's needs and preferences within these, and by helping the team to plan to meet these needs with particular reference to assistants.

	Co-ordinator
Individually:	
• Each member of the group has a set of cards to sort into three piles. These are 　*Pile One* 　Approaches to staff development/INSET which you *have* experienced. 　*Pile Two* 　Approaches to staff development/INSET which you have *not* experienced. 　*Pile Three* 　Approaches that need some explanation or you are not sure about.	Make sure everybody has an envelope with a set of cards. (10 minutes)
• Look again at Pile Two and sort these further into 　*Two (a)* 　Have not experienced, but might like to try. 　*Two (b)* 　Have not experienced and do not seem relevant to your work.	 (5 minutes)
Pairs:	
• Share/compare their choices, seek clarification (then fours if the group is big enough). • Think of things experienced which you would like to try again. • Think of new ideas to you (Pile 2A) • Use the blank cards for any of your own ideas. • Represent you own INSET ideas if they are not amongst the others.	
As a group:	
• Enter into some identification and negotiation about people's needs, preferences and priorities. • Record these on a flipchart. • Within these negotiations identify courses of action for the following: 　- assistants 　- teachers 　- the team as a group 　- INSET Co-ordinators/staff tutor 　- INSET providers.	 (25 minutes)

• Co-ordinator: refer here to the guidance on working out an Action Plan at Level 1 or moving to Level 2.

Now draw up your Action Plan.
Keep the following question in mind:
- Are there any ideas which the team can plan and organise for itself?
- What skills are present within the group to assist this?
- What does the INSET co-ordinator for the school need to know about?
- How will you meet individual needs/team needs through the plan?
- How will you know you have met the needs?

Co-ordinator
Give out individual sheets on action planning
    - outline
    - questions.
Use a big version and a flipchart sheet to agree a plan as a group.

(Action Planning: 30 minutes)

CARD SORTING ACTIVITY

In-service course outside school in working hours.

Staff meeting/professional development meeting in school in working hours.

Negotiations with regard to the contents of the session(s) to be undertaken.

In-service involving
- discussion groups
-workshop tasks
- active involvement.

In-service course counting for a (further) qualification.

In-service involving
- input e.g. lecture
- skills based learning
- demonstration.

A course or series of sessions suggesting tasks to try in the classroom between sessions.

Using 'self-assessment' as a means of identifying require-ment and 'starting points' of the participant.

Feedback session on ideas tried out in the classroom, evaluation of success.

Using development of learning materials as a form of staff development.

Using problem solving as a form of staff development.	Using case studies as a form of staff development.
Using 'role-play' as a form of staff development.	Using 'simulation' as a form of staff development.
Staff development employing content related to your everyday work in the classroom.	Staff development employing content related to an area of work you would like to develop.

Unit 6, Section 2
Co-ordinator's Guidelines

STAFF DEVELOPMENT NEEDS

AIM
To consider what makes staff development (INSET) effective, and examine the possible benefits of assistants and teachers learning together.

MATERIALS NEEDED
- *Before* session give out pre-session notes to *all* participants.
- Flipchart and pens and stand.
- Enough copies of the activity sheets for all participants.
- Copies of the action plan outlines and question sheet for all participants.
- Copies of 'Staff Development Evaluation' exercise, cut and stapled together for each participant.

GENERAL INSTRUCTIONS

> **Total time for activity: 1 hour 30 minutes**

Remind everyone about the aim and their pre-session reading.

Group size:
- Whole group divided evenly into four groups for analysis activity, each with an assistant in them if possible.
- The whole group, for the feedback and action planning.

Accommodation:
- For the analysis activity, space for all group members to see the sheets is important, and for discussion to take place. One or more separate rooms may be helpful.
- The whole group needs to be able to see the flipchart for feedback and Action Planning.

Help in the classroom

Unit 6, Section 2
Pre-Session Notes

LEFT UP IN THE AIR

Classroom assistants should be helped to develop their personal and professional skills alongside other members of staff.

There is much to be gained as a result of exploring ways in which the staff team, teachers *and* assistants, might learn together. Schools have a responsibility to ensure all staff receive appropriate staff development (INSET) opportunities. Indeed they now have budgets that should support 'in-house' staff training. As a result of this policy, most of the required INSET can be experienced in schools, through the staff development plan. Assistants who have recognised a need for further training should not be left condemned to 'feel left up in the air' if their needs are acknowledged in the overall scheme of things in the school.

An assistant here explains the benefit she has gained from school based INSET:

'I've been on two of these professional development days now. The last was about the different ways children learn - it was really interesting. It was originally to do with study skills for GCSE, but everybody decided to think about it for other things. It was very useful. Now, the teacher I work with most and I have been trying out some ideas, when we're working together - trying to make sure everybody's getting access to National Curriculum English by thinking about how they learn best.'

Support to pursue outside sources of INSET should be offered if it is impossible to meet the needs of the assistant within the school. This should also be support in *working* hours, not the assistant's free time.

The activity which follows is aimed at enabling the staff to consider the whole issue of staff development for all of the staff, whether teachers or assistants, as part of an overall plan.

Unit 6, Section 2
Activity Materials

STAFF DEVELOPMENT NEEDS

Classroom assistants should be helped to develop their personal and professional skills alongside other members of staff.

AIM
To consider what makes staff development (INSET) effective, and examine the possible benefits of assistants and teachers learning together.

LEFT UP IN THE AIR

Cameo: An assistant, speculating about staff development she feels is needed:

'If we had a workshop, altogether, led by the science co-ordinator, it would help with the whole business of making sure we're doing the right thing as far as the curriculum is concerned. Neither of *us* was particularly good at school, it would help us to do some practical activities as a group.'

Staff Development (INSET) Evaluation exercise

Individually:
- Each fill in the sheets provided, answering thequestions on each one.
- Use the cameo above to stimulate your thoughts on the matter.
- Do this without chatting to others.

As a group:
- Split into four working groups (pairs or more).
- Each group takes a set of sheets (A,B,C or D).
- *Analyse* what is written on your set of sheets and list what are the main points offered by all the participants' ideas.

Co-ordinator
Make sure everybody has the sheets.

Try to make sure they work individually.
(15 minutes)

Make sure each group has the correct set of sheets to work on.
Each group needs flipchart sheets and pens.

	Co-ordinator
• *Record* these on a single flipchart sheet and choose a spokesperson.	(25 minutes)
• *Feedback* to the whole group your main points.	(25 minutes)

Now draw up you Action Plan.
Some questions to guide your discussion:

• What are the implications for the school staff development plan about which forms of staff development (INSET) this staff group feels are effective?
• How will the assistants' needs be better met?
• How will the teams' needs be better met?
• Are there any ideas which members of the staff can plan and organise for colleagues?
• What skills are present to assist this? and resources?
• From who else, and where else will support be needed?
	Give out individual sheets on action planning
	  - outline
	  - questions.
	Use a big version and a flipchart sheet to agree a plan as a group.
	
	(Action Planning: 25 minutes)

Staff Development (INSET) Evaluation

A. Identify a recent INSET development that you have been in volved in (either as provider *or* receiver) - it can be in or out of school, one day or a series of sessions etc., etc...

What were the actual outcomes for pupils?

B. Identify the strengths of the activity.

Help in the classroom

C. Identify the weaknesses of the activity.

D. Identify the links between the activity and benefits for you and your work in the classroom.

| Assistant | | Teacher |

Identify the links between the activity and benefits for the pupils.

References

Ainscow, M. and Tweddle, D. (1988) *Encouraging Classroom Success* London: David Fulton Publishers.

Ainscow, M. (Ed) (1989) *Special Education in Change* London: David Fulton Publishers.

Ainscow, M. and Muncey, J. (1989) *Meeting Individual Needs* London: David Fulton Publishers,

Barton, L. (1988) *The Politics of Special Education* London: Falmer.

Bollen, R. and Hopkins, D. (1987) *School based review - towards a praxis* Leuven: Acco.

Booth, T., Potts, P. and Swann, W. (1987) *Preventing Difficulties in Learning* Oxford: Basil Blackwell.

Clayton, T. (1990) Welfare assistants: are they equipped for their role? in *Support for Learning* Vol. 5, No. 4, p193-198.

Department of Education and Science (1978) *Special Educational Needs, The Warnock Report* London: HMSO.

Fulcher, G. (1989) *Disabling Policies? A Comparative Approach to Education Policy and Disability* London: Falmer.

Fullan, M. (1982)*The Meaning of Educational Change* Ontario: OISE Press

Fullan, M. (1990) 'Staff development, innovation, and institutional development' in Joyce, B. (Ed) *Changing School Culture Through Staff Development* New York: ASCD.

Fullan, M. (1991)*The New Meaning of Educational Change* New York: Teachers College Press.

Fullan, M. and Park, P. (1981) *Curriculum Implementation* Toronto: Ministry of Education.

Goacher, B., Evans, J., Nelson, J. and Wedell, K. (1988) *Policy and Provision for Special Educational Needs* London: Cassell Educational.

Hargreaves, D. H. et al (1989) *Planning for School Development* London: HMSO.

Hopkins, D. (1987) *Improving the Quality of Schooling* London: Falmer Press.

Hopkins, D. (1989) *Evaluation for School Development* Milton Keynes: Open University Press

Johnson, D. W. and Johnson, R. T. (1989) *Leading the Co-operative School* Edina: Interaction Book Company.

Norwich, B. (1990) *Re-appraising Special Needs Education* London: Cassell.

Reason, P. (1988) *Human Inquiry in Action* London: Sage.

Smith, R. M. (1983) *Learning How to Learn: Applied Theory for Adults* Milton Keynes: Open University Press.

Thousand, J. S. and Villa, R. A. (1991) 'Accommodating for greater student variance, in Ainscow M., *Effective Schools for All* London: David Fulton Publishers.

Tomlinson, S. (1982)*The Sociology of Special Education* London: Routledge.

West, M. and Ainscow, M. (1991) *Managing School Development* London: David Fulton Publishers.

Index